Living Well
with
Chronic Illness

Joanna J. Charnas, LICSW, LCSW

For information, contact
MSI Press
1760-F Airline Highway, #203
Hollister, CA 95023

Copyediting by Mary Ann Raemisch

Cover designed by Carl Leaver

Library of Congress Control Number 2014955563

ISBN: 9781933455150

*For my brother, Charles N. Charnas,
for our childhood*

Joanna J. Charnas, LICSW, LCSW

Acknowledgments

I want to thank the following people for their support of this book: My parents, Stephen Charnas and Suzy McKee Charnas; my uncle, Jonathan Charnas; my brother and sister-in-law, Charles N. Charnas and Margaret Charnas; my godmother, Meryl Cohen; and my surrogate aunt, Sheila Hochman.

Thanks to the following friends: Candace Bremond, Jay Clark, Jeff Clellen, Linda Ealy, Dr. Ronald Elesh, Pieter Estersohn, Dr. Dana Grossman, Kelly Hahn, Grace Hamada, Daniel Hays, Jeffrey King, Diana Macias, Mrs. Careth Reid, Roxanne Rosemire, Dr. Matthew Schumacher, Roberta Strebel, Aaron Tandy, Stella Uruchurtu, and David Wood.

I want to extend special thanks to my editor, Cathy A. Kodra, and to the late Harry R. Nasson II, the latter of whom often sang, "Every day she writes the book" to me as I typed the first draft.

Joanna J. Charnas, LICSW, LCSW

Contents

In February, 2015, The Institute of Health changed the name of Chronic Fatigue Syndrome to Systemic Exertion Intolerance Disease (SEID). The new name is not yet in common usage, so to avoid confusion, it has not been used in this book.

Joanna J. Charnas, LICSW, LCSW

Introduction

When I woke up that morning, I knew something was terribly wrong. I could feel it throughout my body. A week after returning home from my freshman year of college, I'd gone to bed feeling fine. Now, it seemed as though I had the flu. I was weak. I ached from head to toe, and I couldn't seem to focus my thoughts. Strangely, I didn't have any other flu symptoms. I rushed to my doctor, but he couldn't find anything wrong with me. He implied my symptoms might be caused by a mental health crisis instead of a physical problem. This seemed plausible enough. I'd had a stressful first year of college, and my life back at home was a train wreck. I didn't care what caused the problem. I only wanted to feel better. So, I found a psychotherapist who I hoped would help me. Instead, the psychotherapist informed me that my symptoms had nothing to do with the life stressors I was slogging through. What was I supposed to do?

I didn't know it then, but my life had changed forever. After that summer, my health fluctuated from mysteriously awful to somewhat manageable. It was, however, never good. My friends and family all understood I had some kind of weird thing wrong. Occasionally, I had brief periods of vigor, but more often, I felt lousy. I suffered through frequent colds and flus. Sick more frequently than other people I knew, I also became more debilitated than they were by the same illnesses. The office cold that kept my colleagues home for a day or two kept me in bed for at least a week. And to make matters worse, I had a laundry list of other, smaller maladies: severe insomnia, chronic yeast infections, a hormonal imbalance, and eczema, among others. I was a mess.

I always used up all my sick time at work and often tested the patience of my friends and roommates, who could not understand why I was so sick when I didn't have symptoms they could see. I struggled to maintain the basic framework of a normal life with friends, romances, and work. But the outer appearance of my life didn't reveal the full truth. When I wasn't at work or socializing, I often lay in bed at home, so incapacitated I could barely summon the energy to brush my teeth.

As the years went by, I continued to search for a diagnosis and treatment from countless doctors, but none of them could tell me what was wrong with me, a situation both maddening and depressing. After a while, I stopped looking for medical answers and instead learned to adapt to my mystery illness. I focused on maintaining a healthy lifestyle and plunged into many kinds of alternative treatments. None had any real or lasting impact on my health.

The year I turned thirty-six, my worst fears came true. Acutely ill again, I sometimes felt so weak in the morning I struggled just to wash my hair. I often fell asleep on the subway on the way to work, even after a full night's sleep. I dragged myself through the workday and could barely function at my job. When not at work, I spent most of my time lying on the couch at home. I couldn't stand it anymore. I'd had enough. I needed to find out why I was so sick.

Later that year, an Infectious Disease Specialist finally diagnosed me with Chronic Fatigue Immune Deficiency Syndrome, also known as CFIDS, or Chronic Fatigue Syndrome. The infectious disease specialist explained that medical professionals diagnose CFIDS by ruling out all other medical possibilities, the same way they diagnose Alzheimer's disease. No diagnostic test for it existed, nor was there a cure or even standardized treatment. I also learned almost all of the other medical problems I had frequently co-occurred with CFIDS. I had sought answers, but I hadn't expected *this* answer. I was appalled.

I wanted to be diagnosed so I could be treated and recover. Instead, I found out that I had a serious illness, and I could do almost nothing about it. The only relief from my diagnosis was that, after seventeen years of living with a mystery illness, at least I knew what was wrong with me. I needed to put on my big girl pants and deal with it.

But then something strange and unexpected happened. After my diagnosis of CFIDS, I suddenly began to have new kinds of conversations with my friends. For years, I'd had several friends who had chronic illnesses like multiple sclerosis and Crohn's disease. These friends began to share their deepest struggles with me. They'd never opened up to me like this before, and I felt as though I had unknowingly joined a special club. My friends seemed to understand instinctively that I was now one of them. These conversations were surprisingly similar, regardless of the illnesses. We were all fighting to create lives as normal as possible while also managing the limitations illness had forced on us. I discovered we used the same kinds of coping strategies in order to remain as healthy as possible. It didn't matter if my friend had a physical illness or a mental illness. We had all been enrolled in the same club, a deeply comforting realization.

My family and healthy friends did their best to support me as I adjusted to my relapse and diagnosis. They sent me books and articles and said all the right things, but I often felt painfully alone. The only people who truly understood what it was like to be this sick were my friends who also had chronic illnesses. They were the only people in my life able to ease my loneliness.

I wrote this book in order to help people like me who are struggling with chronic illness. I want to share what I've learned from my experiences and what I'm still in the process of learning. I hope this book will help readers cope with some of the challenges of living with chronic illness. I hope it will ease their loneliness. I offer it with love and in the spirit of kinship.

Part I
Emotional Issues

Joanna J. Charnas, LICSW, LCSW

1

Sadness, Hope, Fear, and Other Unexpected Feelings

I knew I'd hit some primal wellspring of grief when I started weeping one morning while watching *Good Morning America*. The announcer listed winners from the previous night's Emmy Awards. The scenario sounded something like this:

"Camryn Manheim for *The Practice*." The television flashed to a picture of the actress, radiant in her finery and success.

Me: Boo, hoo, hoo.

"Andre Braugher for *Homicide: Life on the Street*."

Me: Sob, sniffle, sob, sob.

I'm sure I looked ridiculous. I kept thinking, I don't even care about the Emmys. Sob, sob, sob. But I let go and allowed myself to cry, knowing my feelings needed a release. In retrospect, I think the strong emotions of the winners triggered some of the strong emotions I'd been holding in. At the time, I only knew I needed to let go of my sadness, and it didn't matter what triggered its release. I had many similar crying jags during that time of my life.

Living with chronic illness can evoke many feelings we don't expect and now have to face. It's important not to fight against your emotions. Don't be ashamed of your feelings or believe they must make sense. Experience them, and try not to repress them in the guise of being brave or strong. It's all right to feel whatever emotions exist in the moment. We all know that pretending we aren't feeling something painful doesn't make the bad feeling go away. Those feelings will only go underground and fester if we don't feel them when we should. They can end up making us depressed, anxious, or angry. Feel what you need to feel in the moment.

Otherwise, the emotions will pop up in other forms, at other times, and not necessarily when you're alone in your home watching the morning news.

SADNESS

Sometimes, living with chronic illness can make us feel deeply sad. It's okay to occasionally fall apart. Cry if you need to. After a painful and unexpected episode of particularly bad health, I often found myself overcome by sadness and despair. I would be doing the dishes, making the bed, or watching a television commercial, and I'd start to weep. On top of everything else, I then felt stupid. But so what? No one besides you cares if you sob while you wash the dinner dishes!

However, if sadness overwhelms you and you can rarely shake it off, you may be clinically depressed. Then you might consider consulting a therapist for counseling or antidepressant medications. Therapy and/or medication won't ensure your happiness, but they may alleviate the oppressive quality of your sadness.

While it's natural to feel sad, try not to dwell on your despair longer than necessary. Only you know how long you need to focus on your sad feelings. But if you find yourself weeping as I did that morning while watching TV, once you've stopped crying, try to do something different. Make a conscious effort to shift your mood so you can enjoy the rest of your day, such as

- taking a walk if you are well enough;
- calling a loved one;
- watching a movie at home or in a theater;
- reading;
- stroking the fur of a loved animal; or
- listening to music.

Do anything that soothes and centers you. If your illness circumscribes what you can do, spend five minutes sitting still and breathing deeply if you can. Feel whatever you need to feel, but then try to move on so the difficult emotions don't ruin your day.

FEAR

Coping with fear is one of the most challenging aspects of living with chronic illness. It's easy and understandable to be fearful when you're ill. Unfortunately, fear is like a nasty weed: It may crop up whenever conditions are fertile, and it grows quickly. I easily become afraid whenever I become sick if I don't feel better within a few days. I fear the few days will become a week or even two. If I continue to feel ill, I then fear the relapse will become more severe or that it will be even worse than previous ones. Then, I start to worry about my ability to work, to have relationships, and to do all the things in life I enjoy or value. I am anxious by nature, so none of this is good.

After thirty-five years of living with a chronic illness, I've not been able to let go of fear, and I have no easy answers for how avoid it. However, I try to be disciplined in my thinking. I literally say to myself things like, "Think about something else," or "Don't focus on that." I'm not denying my fear. I'm simply trying not to focus on it once I've acknowledged that's how I'm feeling. I know if I dwell on my fears, I waste valuable energy—energy better spent on being as physically, mentally, and spiritually healthy as possible. This is easier in theory than in practice, but I keep working on it.

When you're afraid, try to figure out what you can do during that particular day to feel better, such as

- reaching out to a friend or family member for support or guidance;
- letting loved ones help you calm down;
- trying to stay in the moment as much as possible and doing your very best in that moment; and/or
- praying for guidance and strength to get to the next moment.

BLAME

It's easy to blame your illness or medical condition on everything that isn't perfect in your life. Avoiding this type of blame may take bedrock honesty if your health severely limits your daily life. Instead of blaming my health for my shortcomings, I think my illness has given me a deeper understanding and acceptance of myself. I am a high-strung, loud, somewhat eccentric person just as much when I'm feeling great as when I'm sick. My illness hasn't enhanced or diminished these qualities. I was well on my way to my present personality by adolescence. My illness didn't create these personality traits, and good health won't make them automatically go away. I'm still working to be the best person I can be. I try to talk less, listen more, and be calmer in general. I know that no matter what happens to my health, I'll have to continue to work on these aspects of my personality. So,

- be honest with yourself;
- take full responsibility for yourself;
- embrace all that is good in you, and
- don't blame your illness for the parts of your personality you want to change.

GUILT

When I was fourteen years old, my mother told me guilt was a completely useless emotion and a waste of energy. She advised me to try to avoid it. Mom was right. Illness may impose limitations on you that you can't always anticipate or control, so it's easy to feel guilty when you believe these limitations have caused you to let someone else, or even yourself, down.

Although it's not easy to practice, try to do your best in every situation. Specifically,

- avoid looking back;
- don't second-guessing yourself;
- be at peace with your efforts; and
- try not to torture yourself over the impact your limitations impose on your life.

If you can't make it to your daughter's sports event, for example, make a big fuss over her when she returns home after the game. If you can't attend an important family birthday party, order a thoughtful gift online. Figure out what you're able to do, and then do your best to follow through. This will help you avoid or release guilt. By focusing on guilt, we remain stuck. By letting go of guilt, we open up emotional and intellectual space for creative solutions.

HOPE

Never give up hope that your health may someday improve. There are numerous stories about people who have suffered from painful and debilitating conditions for years, even decades, and who then have gotten better. In my career as a social worker, I've encountered clients with advanced AIDS who my colleagues and I were convinced were about to die. They didn't die and instead stabilized, returning to better health and leading more functional lives.

I have a friend, Phil, who was diagnosed with HIV in 1988 when many people considered an HIV diagnosis a death sentence. Almost immediately after the diagnosis, Phil went on AZT, the only drug available to treat HIV at the time. Phil told me he hoped AZT would help him stay healthy until another better drug came along. About a year later, the AZT began to make him anemic, so he had to stop taking it. In 1991, he began taking DDI, a new drug that hadn't been available in 1988. When Phil started DDI, he told me the same thing he'd said when he went on AZT: He hoped it would be a bridge to the next, better drug.

In 1996, an entire new class of drugs called protease inhibitors became available to fight HIV. Phil was lucky; he was alive and still healthy. He began taking the new drugs immediately, and he's still doing well on them today. He never gave up hope, even when he had good reason to feel hopeless. Phil has always maintained a positive attitude, even when friends were dying all around him. He's my role model for staying optimistic and for living gracefully with illness. Whenever I feel hopeless, I remember Phil's courage, and it restores my hope. He's my champion and hero.

FRUSTRATION

Being sick is often enormously frustrating. For most of my adult life, at least twice a year, I relapsed or caught a cold or flu that kept me at home for a couple of weeks. Putting my life on hold for an unknown length of time frustrated me tremendously. Not knowing exactly when my immune system would kick in so I could resume my normal life left me feeling anxious and irritable. During these episodes, I treated myself like a pampered diva. Like me, you could

- indulge in as many creature comforts as you can afford;
- read trashy magazines;
- watch endless movies on pay-per-view; and/or
- eat expensive food.

In short, do everything you can within reason and your budget to decrease the frustration of being sick and stuck at home.

I've also often become frustrated with my medical providers and with the bureaucracies I've had to deal with when I've been sick. One of my most frustrating experiences with a doctor took place in the summer of 2003 when I had a bad relapse. I was on partial, short-term disability, working four to six hours a day, for four weeks. My doctor's office submitted my disability paperwork to the state disability office three times, each time either incompletely or inaccurately. Every time office personnel filled the form out incorrectly, the state disability office sent it back to me for corrections. When I called my doctor's office to discuss the corrections, I had to speak to a receptionist and then wait for a return call from my doctor's nurse. I was never allowed to talk directly with my doctor. I found the whole situation maddening! It seemed outrageous and unfair. I wished I had a case manager, parent, or partner to handle the matter, but I didn't have anyone to help me. During this process, I sometimes wept in frustration. I wanted to scream at the staff at my doctor's office. Instead, I summoned my energy and tried to remain persistent but poised. It took all of my self-control to behave politely. I finished short-term disability on July 2, but my paperwork didn't get straightened out until September, when I finally received my last disability check. When the final check arrived two months late, I was proud of myself for keeping my composure during the process.

Frustration is like all the other unexpected emotions we must cope with when we're sick. We have to breathe through it. We have to pace ourselves when faced with frustrations caused by our illness. We need to remember to be kind to ourselves. I cope by praying for wisdom and fortitude, and I reassure myself that I've dealt with similar situations in the past and eventually received what I needed. You have complete control of how you handle your frustration. Don't give in to your worst impulses when you feel this way. When your situation has improved or resolved, you'll feel proud you handled your frustrations with poise and persistence.

~

Being sick is often overwhelming. Sometimes, it's hard to remember life will go on whether or not we're sick. It's easy to forget change is one of the few constants we can count on. Even when I was sickest, many good things happened in my life. I made new friends. The children in my life grew older. Being a part of their lives, as well as the simple act of loving them, made me happy. When I relapsed in 1996, I had a job I loved. I was afraid I would lose it because I missed so much work, but I managed to hold on to it because of a generous and understanding employer. The particular work I did gave me joy beyond any job satisfaction I could have imagined. When an opportunity arose to visit Italy, through a small miracle I was briefly well enough to take the trip, satisfying a long-time dream. None of these things had anything to do with my illness.

These happy, good things often happened at times when my health was terrible, and I frequently felt scared and miserable. Even though sometimes it seemed as if I was spinning my wheels and not making any progress toward regaining my health, all of these joys were also in my life. I didn't let the sadness and frustration about my health take them away from me.

Even if your health remains poor, your life will move forward. No matter what, try to remember there is still good in your life and to enjoy it.

Bad health creates all kinds of difficult feelings. We must accept them, experience them honestly and fully, and then move on. That's the best way to live with our illnesses and remain emotionally healthy.

Joanna J. Charnas, LICSW, LCSW

2

Attitude!

I raced to finish my afternoon errands as I drove through Cambridge, Massachusetts, before the stores closed for the day. Everything had taken much longer than I'd expected. I felt rushed and annoyed, when I suddenly realized the Harvard-Yale football game had just let out. People streamed into the street, and four lanes of traffic quickly became two that were barely moving. I crept along, trying to avoid all the exuberant fans who strolled blithely through the streets and between cars.

As I inched forward in the traffic, I became anxious about making it to the next store on time. The football fans who were keeping me from reaching my destination irritated me. We've all been there—rushed, angry, and stuck in our cars.

Sitting in my car and fuming, I realized I was making myself crazy. I did a reality check and asked myself how important it was to finish my errands. I had to admit my life wouldn't fall apart if I arrived late at my next destination and found the store closed. I questioned if stewing in my car helped me in any way, and I conceded, reluctantly, that it didn't.

I decided I didn't want to stay angry, so instead of continuing to fume, I tried to calm down. I breathed deeply and repeatedly. I tried to find some cheerful music on the radio and focused on not killing any happy football fans. I consciously chose to rescue myself from my own negativity. I checked my bad attitude and took control of it.

You are also in control of your attitude. It's the single most important factor you bring to your health challenges. Your attitude is King, Queen, Zeus, and the Sun God all rolled into one because it influences everything you do and feel about your illness. It dictates how you approach your medical problems. I know people who have minor medical issues who never stop whining and other people who live with life-threatening chronic illnesses who don't complain at all. The latter group approaches every day cheerfully and with a smile. Having a good attitude when we live with illness makes our lives easier, so we need to cultivate the best possible attitude. A bad attitude keeps us stuck in hopelessness, fear, and bitterness. A good attitude propels us toward health and focuses on the positive. It helps us laugh at ourselves and learn from our mistakes instead of obsessing about them. Some tools for this include

- cognitive behavioral therapy;
- positive cognitive restructuring; and
- the tenets of Tae Kwon Do.

GROUP THERAPY

If you wish to improve your attitude about your health, you may want to consider therapy. As a licensed therapist, I believe group therapy may be helpful when learning to reshape your attitude. A good therapy group will help you be honest with yourself and assist you in examining your current attitude. A group of people guided by a competent therapist and working toward similar goals can often help you make the changes you're seeking.

COGNITIVE BEHAVIOR THERAPY

Cognitive behavioral therapy is a specific form of therapy I recommend to people who want to improve their attitudes. You may receive cognitive behavioral therapy either in a group setting or during individual counseling. There are many different schools of cognitive behavior therapy, but they all have the same fundamental principles. They teach you how to examine your thinking in order to restructure negative thoughts into positive or neutral ones (Greenberger and Padesky 1995).

POSITIVE COGNITIVE RESTRUCTURING

I often use *positive cognitive restructuring*, a tool of cognitive behavioral therapy (Greenberger and Padesky 1995), on myself whenever I feel stuck in negativity. Sometimes I'm so cranky, I'm beyond help! I need to let time pass in order to regain my equilibrium. But positive cognitive restructuring often saves me from my worst self, the way it did the day of the big game.

With a good attitude, you can think of yourself as a samurai in pursuit of better health. You become more willing to try new treatment options. Exploring new treatment means you have not resigned yourself to your present health. You're choosing to be hopeful about a healthier future. At times, you will probably need to take a break from this effort, and that's normal and understandable. Your life would become too stressful if you only focused on implementing new medical options. Engaging in new medical regimens takes emotional and physical energy. It is fine to coast with an existing but insufficient medical and/or holistic regimen temporarily as long as waiting won't make you sicker or frailer. This should be a respite, not a resignation to your illness.

TAE KWON DO

I use the five tenets of Tae Kwon Do, a Korean martial art, to structure my attitude. The tenets guide the practice of this sport, but they also offer an elegant template for shaping an effective attitude. The tenets are as follows:

- courtesy;
- integrity;
- perseverance;
- self-control; and
- indomitable spirit.

When you feel you're in a rut, these five tenets may help you move toward a better attitude. I've kept them framed in my office for over twenty years as a constant reminder of how I want to think, feel, and behave.

~

Having a good attitude not only makes your life and the lives of the people around you easier, it's also something you're able to control, even when your body feels out of control. No matter how sick I am, illness doesn't dictate my attitude. So every day, I work hard to maintain a good attitude because it helps make my life more pleasant and allows me to choose how I want to live.

3

Hard Decisions,
Mistakes, and Choices

What was I doing, sitting on the floor in a short, white skirt in the jury room of the Boston courthouse? I'd lost my mind. I'd been called for jury duty and badly wanted to serve. I thought if I dressed up a little, I might improve my chances. I hadn't been feeling well, but I disregarded this in my desire to sit on a jury. I put on my knee-length skirt and sweater set and merrily set off.

The chairs in the jury-pool room were hard and uncomfortable. I sat there for a long time. After a couple hours, I began to feel lightheaded and weak. This should've been my clue to request dismissal from the jury pool. Instead, I thought I might feel better if I put my feet up, so I rested them on an empty chair. That didn't help. I continued to feel worse and began having trouble sitting up. Other people were sitting on the floor, so in my short, winter-white outfit, I lowered myself and leaned against the wall. I felt completely stupid, plopped down on the linoleum in my short white skirt. Instead of asking permission to leave, I stuck it out until 2:00 p.m. when all the potential jurors were excused. Going to jury duty that day was a poor decision. If I'd been thinking clearly at all, I would have requested a deferment.

DECISIONS

We can never anticipate all the decisions we must make once we're sick: treatment decisions, work-related decisions, and smaller daily decisions—the list is endless. Most of these decisions are challenging, and some of them are painful.

Mundane Decisions

Sometimes, the decisions we make seem mundane. I once started a new job the day my uncle was in town on business. He wanted to have dinner with me the first two nights on the job. Completely wiped out both days, I went to dinner with him anyway, even though I knew it might make me so exhausted I'd need days to recover. I did this to myself because I adore my uncle and wanted to make him happy. This was a simple decision, and like many everyday, health-related decisions, it had become ingrained in the fabric of my life. Making up your mind about such a trivial matter may seem easy, but not when you must consider the impact your decision will have on your health. And the decisions never get easier. Living with chronic illness forces us to be thoughtful about many simple matters and often brings small issues into sharp focus. This is a challenging way to live, but it's our reality, and we have to accept it to maintain our emotional equilibrium and maximize our good health.

Life-Altering Decisions

Some decisions are life altering. Since I was a teenager, I wanted to have children. I didn't marry until I was thirty-five, and I was eager to start a family once my husband and I settled into married life. Just when we might have begun a family, I became terribly ill and decided not to have children after all. This came as a harsh realization of my limitations, but I knew I wasn't well enough to take care of a child. I could barely meet my own basic needs. Letting go of something I'd wanted so badly was extraordinarily hard, but it was also easy. I knew having a child would be unfair to the child and my husband, and the demands of motherhood would have made me much sicker. I've never questioned whether I made the right decision in giving up my chance to be a mother. I know I did the right thing. Sometimes, I still cry about that lost chance, but I'm at peace with it.

Decisions about Work

According to *The Oxford Dictionary of Quotations*, Freud said, "All that matters is love and work" (1999). Sometimes we have to make tough decisions about one or the other. I like to work (talk of decisions regarding love will come later in this book), and I'm committed to the values and practice of social work. When I decided not to have children, my career became even more important to me. Most of the people I know who live with a chronic illness want to work, and we struggle to stay employed. Not working has financial ramifications, of course, but it also may engender a significant emotional loss. When we stop working, we may feel we've lost a vital part of our identity and our sense of self-worth. When I thought I might not be able to work full time, I felt frantic and unmoored from the bedrock of my life.

Giving up work may make us feel we're no longer productive members of society. Being unable to support ourselves as we're accustomed to can be devastating. In the mid to late 1990s when I was sickest, I struggled to stay employed. I went to work even when I was very ill. I know I made myself much sicker by clinging to my forty-hour workweek. I should've reduced my work hours or taken a few months off to rebuild my strength. (I did reduce my hours a couple of times during that period, but only for four to six weeks—not long enough to make a significant difference in my general health.)

After three years of agonizing over this issue, I asked my employer if I could reduce my hours permanently, but only by eight hours a week. The agency I worked for agreed to the decrease in hours, but this didn't last long because I, along with ten percent of the staff, was laid off a few months later.

I'll never be sure if I made the right decision by continuing to work full time during that period of my life. I believe that going to work every day, sick or not, was critically important to my emotional well-being. I know many people who've wrestled with this dilemma. Some have decided to leave work, and some have struggled to remain employed. These are incredibly tough decisions.

Good Decisions and Bad Decisions

Applaud your good decisions whenever you can. I wanted to go to Italy for years, and in 1997, my father asked me to join my stepmother and him on a trip to Florence. I had no idea if I could manage the rigors of international travel or if I'd have the energy for the hustle and bustle of visiting a new city. The last time I'd traveled to Europe, I'd been stuck in bed, sick, for most of my five days in Scotland. I watched Scottish soap operas instead of touring the countryside as planned. I didn't want a repeat of that experience, but I also didn't want to pass up the chance to see Italy! I decided a little bit of Florence would be better than none and resigned myself to the possibility that I might need to spend half of every day resting. I decided I could live with this compromise, but I still worried whether I'd be healthy enough to make the trip. Luckily, when the time came, I felt well enough to travel. To my surprise, I felt fine for the entire trip and had a great time. My gamble paid off, and I was pleased with myself for deciding to take the risk.

At other times, I've made poor decisions. In the fall of 2000, I went away for several weekends in a row and found myself more worn out than I could have possibly imagined. I'd been feeling so well that I simply forgot I couldn't handle a certain level of activity. I indulged in happy, happy denial, and, as a result, I paid the price of profound exhaustion for weeks afterward.

MISTAKES

You're going to make decisions about your health you'll later think of as mistakes. Making mistakes is part of the process of learning to live with illness. There's no point in beating yourself up about it. Living with illness is always a challenge: *Can I handle this, or can't I? Will this make me feel worse, or will I be all right?* If you don't make any decisions you later realize were mistakes, then you're only doing what feels completely safe and are never pushing your limits. Testing your limits is part of the ongoing process of learning how to live with illness.

No-Regret Zone

I try to live in what I refer to as the "no-regret zone." Don't be regretful about poor decisions. If we learn from them, then even poor decisions have positive and useful outcomes. The lessons we learn from mistakes help us shape better decisions in the future.

Joanna J. Charnas, LICSW, LCSW

Before my current job at the local naval hospital, I worked on its psychiatric wards. After I started the new job, I ran into one of my former patients, a man of considerable rank, while I was taking my mid-day stroll around base. I'd done a lot of supportive counseling with this man and knew him well. He stopped to chat with me and admitted he was going downhill emotionally. He had a great outpatient therapist and psychiatrist, so I encouraged him to ask for an emergency appointment if he felt suicidal, which he had in the past. Sure enough, a few days later I found out he'd been hospitalized again. After clearing the visit with his therapist, I went to the acute psychiatry ward to see him. The patient told me he'd been feeling better, and so he'd decided to stop taking his medication for bipolar disorder. He admitted he'd made a bad decision. I asked him what he'd learned from his most recent hospitalization, and the patient said he learned he must stay on his medications no matter how good he feels. I applauded his insight and urged him not to forget it. He hasn't been admitted again since this incident occurred.

A Process of Fine-Tuning

Making good decisions is a process of fine-tuning. The decisions don't change, but we keep refining our responses to them. For example, I have to decide what, if anything, to tell employers about my health every time I change jobs. Do I tell my new employer nothing about my health problems and hope I stay healthy, making the topic irrelevant? Or do I give him a clue about my health issues, so if I get sick, it's not a complete surprise? Even before I received a formal diagnosis, I'd tried both approaches. It's not one decision. It's a new decision every time I have a new employer and a process that becomes a bit more refined each time I change jobs.

Living Well with Chronic Illness

Every day we need to make decisions about our health and matters affecting our health. I've learned you can let go of important parts of your life or certain dreams for the future, and still be happy. But it's also normal and natural to be sad about these decisions and to mourn your losses. The best we can do is applaud our good decisions, learn from the bad ones, laugh about them, and move on.

CHOICES

Choices are kissing cousins to decisions. If you're making decisions, then you have choices in your life. In the face of illness, choice is a gift, even if it feels like a burden. Be grateful for the choices you *can* make. Remember that illness has not taken away our ability to make choices even in our constricted lives. Knowing this helps ward off feelings of powerlessness and boosts good mental health.

I'm grateful I always had a choice about whether I should work and how much to work. I'm glad I never became so sick that this choice was taken away from me. Whether I made good decisions or bad ones along the way, at least I enjoyed the privilege of weighing my options.

~

The consequences I have experienced in life have been the result of my choices, not those imposed on me by illness. In my sanest, calmest moments, I am always profoundly grateful for this.

Joanna J. Charnas, LICSW, LCSW

4

Looking Good, Feeling Good: Your Body Image

I was not prepared or happy when my therapist instructed me to give myself weekly pedicures. In my mid-twenties at the time, I had always felt I had big, broad peasant feet, genetically designed to till the soil. I'd never paid much attention to caring for my feet or hands and was generally a no-makeup, no-muss-or-fuss kind of girl. When I first attempted to complete my assignment, I smeared nail polish all over myself: little drips on my feet, my hands, and any exposed skin. I struggled mightily to learn this new skill, and, over time, I gradually got the hang of it.

Then people began to compliment my feet. Several people even commented that I should become a foot model. Completely taken aback by the attention and compliments, I began to enjoy my pretty, colorful toenails. No matter how sick I was, I always felt like Joan Crawford from the ankles down.

Being sick may make us feel bad about our bodies. Sometimes illness disfigures us or causes physical pain. It's easy to become angry with our bodies for being sick. We may even begin to think of our bodies as separate from our true, or core, selves. While there is something to be said for the idea of the body being the house of the soul, I prefer to think of the mind, body, and spirit as one entity with three different expressions.

APPEARANCES

When we're sick, it's important to feel as good as we can about our bodies in order to maximize our mental health. Hating any part of ourselves is harmful. We need to remember that we are one integrated system and to love our bodies even though they've changed or made our lives more challenging than they used to be.

It's easy to neglect our bodies or pay less attention to them because we feel they have betrayed us by becoming sick. Without meaning to, we might let our appearance go. This behavior may lead to a vicious cycle of self-neglect, only making us feel worse about ourselves than we already do.

One way to be as emotionally healthy as possible when we're sick is to love our bodies despite their challenges. Enhance every possible part of your body to optimize your ability to feel good about it. Dress as well as your budget and energy allow. In my early forties, while shopping at a discount store, a friend encouraged me to buy a shapeless, gray chenille bathrobe. Even though it was size 3X and I was size 14, she said her partner had one and that I would love how comfortable it felt. So, I bought it. When I wore it, I looked like a large, furry sea creature had crawled out of the ocean, enveloped my body, and died there. But it *was* amazingly comfortable! I continued to wear it even after I burned one of the sleeves. I have floor to ceiling mirrors on my bedroom closet doors. Whether I want to or not, I can't help seeing myself. One day as I was opening the closet door, I had an *Aha!* moment and thought, why am I wearing this dreadful thing? I have an hourglass figure and look best when I show it off. So, I trashed my burned bathrobe, trotted out to Macy's, and treated myself to a china-blue, floral, belted bathrobe. I had allowed myself to look dumpy unnecessarily. I could have felt pretty as I ate my morning oatmeal instead of looking like a furry troll. I won't make that mistake again.

If your body has changed significantly because of your illness, or if you're living a considerably different kind of life because you're sick, find clothes that make you feel good about yourself and work for your appearance and needs *now*. Don't get sloppy and neglect yourself. Don't ever let yourself feel dumpy, and never leave your house and present yourself to the world that way. Everyone has the potential to look and feel attractive. Help keep your spirits high by looking your best.

I stopped regularly painting my toenails years ago. I no longer need the therapeutic lift it gives me. But whenever I feel bad about my body, I know at least one way I can boost myself up again, and I treat myself to a professional pedicure. Try to figure out what is going to make you feel good about your body, and then pay attention to that part of yourself. Our bodies are not the enemy. It's important for our emotional well-being to feel as positive about them as we can.

PHYSICAL CAPABILITIES

Sometimes, feeling good about our bodies relates to our physical capabilities. Many of us don't have the physical capacity we once did. In my early thirties, I attended Tae Kwon Do classes twice a week. There were very few women in my classes, usually only one or two others, so I was learning, training, and sparring mostly with men. I called it "kicking butt with the big boys." Often the men were much larger and stronger than me. I had to be in excellent shape to keep up with them. While participating in Tae Kwon Do, I wasn't always healthy. Often, I missed weeks of class at a time, but when I was well enough, I worked out hard in class. I loved Tae Kwon Do, and I was halfway to earning my second-degree black belt when I stopped. Now, I'm not well enough to engage in such a strenuous form of exercise.

Although I mourned the passing of this wonderful episode of my life, I try to embrace the exercise I can still enjoy. When I'm feeling well, I take daily, twenty-minute walks during the workweek. I also have a walking buddy and take an hour-long walk with her once a week, and, if I'm up to it, I throw in another hour-long walk during the weekend. This is all I can tolerate without over exerting myself, making myself sick. Although I can't study Tae Kwon Do anymore, I love my walks and the feeling of my legs working hard. It's not what I used to do, but it's still something that makes me happy.

~

After you have mourned your losses, try to embrace the present and enjoy what your body is still capable of doing.

Part II
Practical Challenges

Joanna J. Charnas, LICSW, LCSW

44

5

Information is Empowering

The first words out of my mouth when I received a diagnosis of Chronic Fatigue Syndrome were, "I can't have that. Those people can't get out of bed." Wrong! The Infectious Disease Specialist gently corrected me and firmly let me know I was now one of "those people." When I left her office, one thing was clear to me: if I was going be as healthy as possible with my new diagnosis, I needed to learn as much as I could about it, and quickly.

One of the best things I did for myself after I received that diagnosis in 1996 was to obtain information about my illness. Information is empowering. The more you know about your illness, the more tools you have to deal with it. Information

- guides you in making good treatment decisions;

- helps you understand what is happening to your body, which gives you a small measure of control and therefore decreases fear and anxiety; and

- makes you a better medical consumer because you will be able to understand your treatment options.

When you arm yourself with information about your illness and treatment options, you're able to talk to your medical provider assertively and confidently.

SOURCES OF INFORMATION

There are several places where you can obtain valuable medical information. Among these are the Internet, patient advocacy groups, support groups, and medical journals.

Internet Resources

The quickest and easiest way to access information is through the Internet. There are many excellent medical sites available to you on the Web. Three good places to start your search for medical information are the WebMD[1], Centers for Disease Control (CDC)[2], and the Mayo Clinic.[3] You may also use a search engine such as Yahoo! or Google to research information about your illness. Start your Internet search by entering the name of your illness and your zip code in the search field to find local resources, such as support groups and organizations that serve people with your condition. Many people have discovered life-saving treatments through these kinds of searches.

Patient Advocacy Groups

Patient advocacy groups are another great place to find medical information. I often refer my patients and their families to The National Alliance on Mental Illness (NAMI)[4], which is a patient-run organization. NAMI offers support groups, literature on various mental illnesses, and a great website. After I received a diagnosis of Chronic Fatigue Syndrome, I joined the Massachusetts CFIDS Society.[5] This organization sent me brochures and a few articles as well as their quarterly newsletter. I continued to subscribe to their newsletter long after I moved to California. I have recommended it to people with Chronic Fatigue Syndrome all over the country. Now I read it online. I never worry about missing a breakthrough, because I know the website will report on any important treatment news. Many national organizations for specific illnesses exist, and they may have helpful and informative pamphlets, brochures, reading lists, and newsletters.

Support Groups

Support groups provide another source of beneficial information. Often, your peers in the community will know more than you do about your illness, particularly if they've been living with it longer than you have. One of the functions of support groups is sharing information. When I first received my CFIDS diagnosis, I ran a support group program for people infected and affected by HIV and AIDS. I knew from my work how important the information sharing that occurs in groups can be.

Medical Journals

Medical journals also offer much helpful literature on illness. At the time I found out I had CFIDS, I worked for an organization that had a medical library. I asked the librarian, a sweet and kind man named Eric, if he would help me find citations on articles about Chronic Fatigue Syndrome. Eric not only looked up the citations, but he also pulled the articles from the journals, copied them, read the articles, and underlined significant points for me. I can never thank him enough for his act of generosity and kindness.

When my sister-in-law, Margaret, learned about my diagnosis, she immediately went to a local medical library open to the general population. She asked the librarian to research Chronic Fatigue Syndrome and quickly sent me a large stack of copied articles. Because of the efforts of these two caring people, within a week or so of my diagnosis, I owned a three-inch stack of information about my illness. These articles were extremely helpful to me during that first difficult period following my diagnosis.

PACING INFORMATION INTAKE

While acquiring information is important and empowering, it's also important to consume information at your own speed. Read as much or as little as you can handle. Take a break from educating yourself if you feel overloaded. After reading my first set of newsletters, a book on Chronic Fatigue Syndrome, and a good portion of the articles Eric and Margaret gave me, I put the most medically complex articles in a drawer. They stayed in that drawer for an entire year. If I had forced myself to read them past the point of my ability to absorb information, I might have missed some important issues in the articles.

~

Unless you have a rapidly progressing illness, give yourself time to educate yourself. Pace yourself so that your ability to process and use information constructively remains intact. The information will still be there when you need it.

6

How to Obtain Good Medical Care

When the Patient Relations Representative asked me if she could do anything *else* for me after she resolved my initial complaint, I pounced. "Yes," I replied. "You could transfer me to Dr. B.'s caseload!"

Dr. B. had treated me once when my doctor was unavailable, and his warm bedside manner and attention to detail impressed me deeply. After the appointment, I'd asked my HMO to transfer me to his service but had been informed it was full. Now that the HMO was attempting to assuage me after bungling a different matter, I recognized my opportunity to ask for the transfer again. Sure enough, the Patient Relations Representative transferred me to Dr. B.'s caseload, and instantly I went from having a marginally competent doctor to being in the care of an excellent one.

TRUST

When you're sick, you need to have the best medical care available to you. The most important aspect of your doctor-patient relationship is trust. Unless you have limited options, don't accept anything less. Remember, your physician is helping you achieve optimal health. Your health affects every part of your life, so it's essential to have a doctor whom you trust.

LISTENING AND RESPONDING

Other important aspects of my relationship with my doctor are his ability to listen and respectfully respond to me. I don't want a physician who's dismissive of me or of my illness. I seek doctors who are receptive to my suggestions. If I bring new treatment information to them, I expect them to consider it.

When I moved from Massachusetts to California in 1999 and met my new doctor, I told him I had brought him a copy of my medical record. He clearly wasn't paying attention to me and didn't seem to have any interest in reading it because he handed it back to me at the end of the visit. When I reminded him I'd brought the copy for him to review, he took it, but during my next visit, it became evident that he hadn't read it because he had no background regarding an on-going medical issue of mine. Needless to say, I found a new doctor as soon as possible.

By comparison, Dr. B., my doctor in Massachusetts, was excellent. He remembered my medical history each time I saw him. On occasion, I'd give him articles about Chronic Fatigue Syndrome, with which he had little experience. He always accepted the articles graciously and appeared genuinely interested in learning about my illness. When he and I had a difference of opinion, he would listen to my ideas and compromise.

CONFIDENCE

It's important to trust your feelings about your doctor. It's easy to settle for the first available physician when you're sick and possibly scared, but rely on your instincts.

Don't talk yourself into treatment by a doctor you don't like or in whom you lack confidence. Being sick is challenging enough without adding problems with your doctor into the mix. At a minimum, you need to have faith in your doctor. Of course, there may be exceptions to this. If you have a medical need only one particular physician in your community can meet, you may have to learn to work with this person. Unless you are without alternatives, though, don't subject yourself to ongoing treatment by someone who makes you uncomfortable.

It may take you awhile to find a doctor you like and trust. You might have to go through a process of trial and error in your search for the right physician. This search may be discouraging. However, if you have a chronic illness (versus an acute one), you have the time to find a doctor who will meet your expectations and needs. If you don't like your physician but don't have the energy to find a new one, that's okay. Once your health has stabilized and you've started to feel revitalized, begin your search for a better doctor.

SPECIALISTS

Another important guideline to remember when doctor shopping is to look for a physician who specializes in your illness. For example, if you have AIDS, it's in your best interests to have a doctor whose expertise includes HIV treatment. The more experience your doctor has treating patients with your illness, the more comprehensive, state-of-the-art care you are likely to receive. Even if you love your general practitioner, consider switching your care to a doctor who specializes in your illness, or see a specialist in addition to your general practitioner.

Sometimes, it's not possible to see a specialist. When I received a diagnosis of Chronic Fatigue Syndrome, few doctors in Boston specialized in this disease. Those who did sought patients who perfectly fit the Center for Disease Control's diagnostic criteria for Chronic Fatigue Syndrome because the doctors needed good research subjects. I heard other CFS patients complain about this practice, but it didn't bother me. I *wanted* those physicians to conduct research and find a treatment or cure. I realized that the best kind of doctor I could find for myself was one who would treat me respectfully and who would engage and respond cooperatively.

DECIDING ON THE RIGHT DOCTOR

You'll have to make your own decisions about what you want from your physician and what you're willing to accept. You will base your decisions on a host of factors:

- the medical options in your community;
- your health insurance;
- your access to transportation; and
- multiple other issues specific to your needs.

Any one of these or other factors may require you to compromise on what would be the ideal choice for you. But try not to compromise too much. Look for ways to overcome the obstacles in order to get the right doctor for you.

~

In arranging your medical care, always remember this is a vitally important aspect of your life. Keep your standards as high as possible!

7
Your Body Knows Best: Listen to It!

Sometimes, as much as we would rather do otherwise—having great plans in mind—we just have to listen to our body and take care of ourselves appropriately. Our body gives us signals that help us determine what is best for us at the time. In addition, our body is part of a larger ecosystem that we can use to make sure that we take the best care of ourselves in order to live as well as we can with whatever illness we have.

Signals

I'd been lying in bed trying not to move my throbbing head as I waited for the worst headache of my life to subside. When my husband, Harry, arrived home from work, he blithely pronounced, "Oh, you have a sinus headache."

"Is that what this is?" I whimpered. The pain in my head was overwhelming. For days, I'd been ignoring the signals my body sent me. In only a couple of days, I'd be leaving for New York City where I'd enrolled in an expensive therapy course.

Joanna J. Charnas, LICSW, LCSW

The week before my scheduled departure, I'd become miserably ill with a sinus infection. Initially I went to work, but by the end of the week, I became too sick to do my job. Even after the severity of the infection forced me to stay home, I remained determined to travel to New York and take the course. The fact that I could barely see straight didn't sway me to alter my plans. I even called the training institute to find out if I could lie down during the class breaks and was informed that it had couches where I could rest. In my weak and woozy state, I'd thought that would work.

I'd convinced myself I had a reasonable plan until the headache from hell hit me. That headache, though, helped me "hear" the message my body had been sending me all along: I was much too sick to go to New York. After I recovered from my headache, I canceled plans for the trip and focused on recuperating from the sinus infection, which I should have done in the first place. I still have credit for $470.00 sitting in my desk drawer, dated 1998, from the training institute.

One way to maximize and maintain your good health is to learn to listen to the signals your body sends you. This is not an endorsement to obsess over each little ache, pain, or blotch. However, everyday matters sometimes distract you, and you miss the signals your body sends. You can get out of synch with yourself. This is easy to do. Life is demanding and complex, and it's hard to pay attention to your body all the time. But if you don't listen to the little signals your body sends, it's going to send you increasingly bigger, uglier messages until you react appropriately.

Listening to your signals is often just a matter of knowing your triggers and responding to them. I'm an unusually tidy person. On a scale of one to ten, I'm a good eight, somewhere just below obsessive. When I begin to move up the scale and become irritated by small items that are out of place in my home, it's a clear signal to me that I've overextended myself and need to rest as soon as possible.

I also know when I begin to get cranky that I've overextended myself and need to stop whatever I'm doing and rest. The escalation of my neurosis, or finding I'm short tempered, is always a clear signal to me that I'm at risk of getting sick.

Although I know these things about myself, I don't always pay attention to them. I'm as fully capable of ignoring my body's signals as the next person. I like to think I have a naturally cheerful disposition. I've never had much understanding of people who are prone to crankiness. My attitude toward cranky behavior used to lie somewhere between "get a grip" and "get over it."

My attitude changed one year after I caught the flu. Initially, I called it the Florentine Flu because I'd felt my first flu symptoms on the plane coming home from my trip to Florence, Italy. I went to work immediately after the trip until I became so sick that both my supervisor and the head of my department sent me home, something that has never happened to me before or since.

I stayed home for a week and a half, but even after I returned to work, I still didn't feel quite my usual self. I could drag myself through the workday, but by evening I'd used up every physical and emotional reserve I possessed. Even brief attempts at small talk with Harry overwhelmed me. I'd find myself feeling bad tempered quite suddenly and would need to make a concerted effort just to be minimally pleasant. After I had a chance to relax and reconstitute my energy, my emotional equilibrium would return.

However, sometimes I was so worn out by the time I reached home I couldn't suppress the cranky woman inside my head. This transitional time between work and settling in at home was a veritable coming out party for the Inner Bitch. I went on in this manner for almost two months. I began to call the Florentine Flu the Forever Flu, and I found myself constantly apologizing to Harry for being testy with him. I felt as though an extraterrestrial alien had taken over my body, and I blamed her for the crankiness. I was irritable so often that for the first time in my life I had empathy for cranky people! Accustomed to not feeling well, I had some sense of how to manage my day-to-day health, but adding the residual effects of the flu to the physical demands already on my plate was too much for me.

In hindsight, it's easy to see I simply returned to work too soon. I *completely* ignored all my body's signals in the desire to do my job. It requires time to learn our body's signals. Even when we're able to recognize them, it takes determination as well as trial and error to understand them and take corrective action. They can be easy to ignore, but when you don't pay attention, your health suffers. Begin to listen to your body's signals, and, with practice, you'll learn the best way to respond to them so you can be as healthy as possible.

Your Ecosystem

I like to think of my body as an ecosystem, unique unto itself like a rainforest or the Antarctic. Like these places, much about my body is known by the scientific community, but much also remains a mystery to them. It's up to me to learn what mysteries science cannot yet explain.

For example, often when I catch a cold or the flu, I only have symptoms on one side of my body, usually the right side. I may ache from head to toe, but only my right lung, right nostril, and the right side of my throat are affected. This expression of symptoms is a medical anomaly. Not one of my doctors over the years has been able to explain it to me. It is part of my personal ecosystem, but science cannot explain why.

~

Everyone's body reacts differently, even if someone lives with an illness that's common and well understood by the medical community. As you learn about the unique characteristics of your body, you'll become more adept at listening to it. You can learn to be sensitive to your body's signals in a healthy way in order to maximize your ability to cope with the demands of your illness. Your life will be much happier once you learn to do this!

Joanna J. Charnas, LICSW, LCSW

Take Care of Yourself

In taking care of yourself, the most important thing is to do what works. Consider what works for everyone in achieving wellness, and consider what works for you personally in areas such as eating, exercising, simple pleasures, and other regular activities.

DO WHAT WORKS

"Should I, or shouldn't I?" I stood in front of the newsstand next to my subway stop for over five minutes, debating whether to buy *People* magazine. I always carried a book with me to read on my half-hour subway ride to and from work, but I didn't have the energy to focus on the serious novel I'd brought with me that day. Exhausted from work, I felt a deep longing to peruse the pages of a completely undemanding magazine, to look at the photos and read the captions and maybe a movie review or two. When I got home, I realized how hard I'd been on myself. It dawned on me that I didn't need to make every moment a growth experience. I could read whatever I wanted if it were going to help me unwind from my workday.

Mind Jell-O

My mother had a category of entertainment she labeled "mind Jell-O." Mind Jell-O is easy on our brains the way that real Jell-O is easy on our bodies. It took me until my forties to accept that it's okay for me to indulge in mind Jell-O. I've learned I need to do what works for me in the moment and not set inflexible and often unrealistic standards for myself. These days I embrace many forms of mind Jell-O and have an annual subscription to *People*, which I enjoy immensely.

The need to take care of yourself may seem obvious, but it's easy to dismiss your needs and put someone or something else first. This inevitably backfires because if you don't take care of yourself when you should, you run the risk of becoming sicker. Then, whatever or whomever demands your time, energy, and attention will probably be getting fewer of those things from you. Just remember, like many of the challenges of living with chronic illness, learning to take care of yourself is a process of trial and error.

Doing What Works

Do what works for *you*. This may seem like another obvious piece of advice, but those of us living with chronic illness often talk ourselves out of whatever makes us feel good, the way I did that day at the newsstand. We apply to our current situations the standards we had for ourselves when we were healthy instead of cutting ourselves much-needed slack.

For example, I've heard people living with chronic illness say they feel bad about watching too much television. Everyone knows about the evils of viewing excessive amounts of TV, but when you're sick, it's an entirely different ball game. Then television can be a godsend. I know that when I'm at my worst, even *People* is too challenging for me. I barely have the energy to focus my eyes or mind on the written word. When I'm under the weather, television becomes a welcome distraction. It also helps me feel less lonely during times I'm home alone for days or weeks. Don't feel guilty or judge yourself if you watch countless hours of TV when you're ill. Remember, mind Jell-O is okay. You're simply trying to make it through the day as best you can and with your spirit intact.

There's still such a thing as too much television even when you're ill. I knew I'd been staring at the TV too long one day when I found myself admiring Maury Povich's backside.

"Mmm . . ." I thought. "Maury, that is one good-looking butt you have." I considered this a clear signal that I had slipped from the precarious perch upon which my sanity rested, and I needed to *turn off the television immediately.* But most of the time if we aren't feeling well, it's fine to watch as much television as we want.

Achieve Wellness

When you live with illness, it's as important to maintain your general wellness as it is to adhere to whatever regimen your specific condition requires. It doesn't make sense to attend to the medical demands of your particular disorder while living an unhealthy lifestyle.

The President's Council on Fitness and Sports defines wellness this way: "Wellness is a multidimensional state of being describing the existence of positive health in an individual as exemplified by quality of life and a sense of well-being."[6]

For me, wellness means developing and maintaining habits that allow me to be as healthy as possible on a daily basis. Because there's no standardized treatment for

Chronic Fatigue Syndrome, the only thing I can do to max-imize my health is focus on overall wellness. It's a central and critically important part of my life. Here's a summary of what I try to include in my wellness regimen, and what you might consider incorporating into your daily life, too:

- eating well;
- exercising regularly;
- sleeping enough;
- breathing deeply;
- washing your hands;
- meditating often; and
- drinking enough water.

Eat Well

For most of my life, I've been a little overweight—in the 5-15+ pounds range. It would be easy to assume, at my size, that I eat junk food. Untrue! Except when I'm indulging my sweet tooth, I rarely eat unhealthful foods. I am somewhat religious about maintaining a good diet. (My problem is portion control.) I try to eat fruits and vegetables every day. I stay away from fast food, most processed food, and fried foods. I don't drink alcohol and only drink soda a few times a year. My eating habits may seem severe, but they developed over more than thirty years. I gave up alcohol, except for the occasional toast, when I was twenty-four, and stopped drinking soda when I was thirty-three.

Years ago my goddaughter, Frannie, then five, and her mother, Stephanie, "cat sat" for me during a weekend I was out of town. I told Stephanie that she and Frannie were welcome to snack on anything in the house. When they got to my home, however, they discovered there wasn't any food that would interest a five-year-old. I had nuts, cheese, and crackers, but no cookies, candy, ice cream, chips, or other goodies. I'd rushed to get ready for my trip and hadn't had time to buy any treats for my goddaughter. When I returned home, Stephanie told me Frannie had been disappointed there was nothing yummy in my house for her to snack on. Stephanie marveled at how "cleanly" I ate.

I'm so accustomed to eating well, I hadn't thought about all the things that aren't part of my usual diet until Stephanie mentioned it. The truth is, I feel better when I eat well. If I don't eat enough vegetables, I crave them the way I sometimes crave chocolate. A big salad makes me feel well, and I prefer eating one to a sandwich or burger. Following a nutritious diet helps me stay healthy, so I'm happy to eat that way. If you would like to explore developing healthier eating habits, The Nutrition Source and its Healthy Eating Pyramid[7] might be a good place to start.

Bon appetite!

Exercise Regularly

Exercise is important when we live with chronic illness, as long we're mindful of the reasonable constraints of our condition and not engaging in activities that will make us sicker. Many people don't understand the kind of exercise that's appropriate for people with Chronic Fatigue Syndrome. Forcing those of us who are symptomatic to exercise hard is only going to make us feel worse. This is also true for many people living with other illnesses. But the exercise regimen you choose depends on your specific condition. Consult with your doctor before starting any new exercise program. She may have specific recommendations about what is appropriate and optimal for people living with your illness.

If you are unsure how to start a fitness program, are able to leave the house, and have the financial resources, one way to begin your program is to join a gym and consult with their fitness trainer. The trainer will design a program tailored for your needs and limitations. A less expensive way to start exercising is to join a fitness group, like a club for mall walkers. Or find one friend who will exercise with you. I have a walking buddy, with whom I walk three miles every Monday. Having a standing date to exercise helps me to stick to my fitness goal and not slack. If you have difficulty leaving your house, you might want to explore exercise DVDs to use at home. This is another less expensive and more private option than joining a gym or club.

Some of us are extremely limited in the types of exercise we can do. For example, the morbidly obese, the frail elderly, or people with mobility limitations often can't go to a gym or perhaps even exercise standing up. When I worked for an adult daycare for the frail elderly in the early 1980's, the program participants exercised daily from their chairs. My grandmother, who lived to be one hundred, took a water aerobics class and performed daily stretching exercises before getting out of bed in the morning. She continued this regimen well into her nineties. If you have extreme limitations and are unsure what exercise options to pursue, ask your doctor to refer you to a physical therapist, who can design an exercise program just for you.

In addition, many books are available to guide you in your fitness goals. I've listed two good ones below.

ACSM's Exercise Management for Persons with Chronic Diseases and Disabilities (Durstine et al., 2009)

Recapture Your Health: A Step-By-Step Program to Reverse Chronic Symptoms and Create Lasting Wellness (Stoll & Decourtney, 2006)

Both of these books are available from Amazon.com and have high ratings and glowing reader reviews.

Don't assume because you live with a chronic illness that you cannot be fit. Explore the exercise options available to you and choose one you believe can work for you. By maximizing your fitness, you will feel better and be proud of your efforts, just as I am of mine.

Sleep Enough

When we're sick, sometimes our bodies are so depleted they dictate how much we sleep. Yet, some of us are able to make choices about the amount of we sleep we obtain. At my sickest, I used to joke that I went to bed at the same time as an average seven-year-old—as early as 8:30. I'd come home from work, eat, read a little, maybe watch television, and then crash at an embarrassingly early hour. Now that I'm feeling better, most of my evenings remain quiet, but occasionally I feel energized and go to bed very late, even when I have to work the next day. Having this kind of choice again in my life is wonderful.

The National Sleep Foundation (NSF) states on its website that adults need 7-9 hours of sleep per night. Many pronouncements by the media say Americans suffer chronic sleep deprivation, and according to the NSF, Americans average less than 6½ hours nightly.[8] Good sleep hygiene, though, is vitally important for people living with chronic illness. Our overtaxed bodies pay too high a price for missing sleep. We're already straining to remain functional, so it's unwise for us to deprive ourselves of sleep and make our bodies work harder than needed. Figure out how much sleep you usually require, and then be good to yourself and make sure you go to bed on time.

Many of us living with chronic illness have concomitant sleep problems. I've been a world-class insomniac for as long as I can remember. When all of my classmates in kindergarten were asleep on their mats after lunch, I lay wide awake, staring at the ceiling. When the other campers were happily napping on their beds after lunch at sleepaway camp, I tossed and turned, eager for the rest period to end. Pain and menopause have compounded my sleep problems as I've gotten older.

If you have similar sleep issues, there are several ways to address them. You should start by consulting your doctor. She may order a sleep study for you to find out if there are organic issues, such as sleep apnea, contributing to your sleep problems. You may need a CPAP (continuous positive airway pressure) machine to help you breathe, or a sleep aid in the form of a pill. If you have pain that prevents you from sleeping, you should also address this with your doctor. She may want to tailor your pain medications in ways that facilitate sleep. If you suffer from depression or anxiety, this may also negatively impact your sleep. Although many general practitioners prescribe psychiatric medications, I recommend patients see a psychiatrist for both sleep and psychiatric issues. A psychiatrist will be better informed about medications that address both needs, and he can prescribe the best medicine for them.

It's almost impossible to remain healthy when you are frequently sleep deprived. Seek medical or psychiatric help if needed, and become disciplined in your personal routines. I'm grateful for every night that I sleep soundly and wake refreshed. Whatever the day brings, a good night's sleep will make it better.

Breathe Deeply

We've all seen small children gasp for air when they're distressed. I've often observed this same behavior in my adult mental health patients when they're upset or out of control. During those times, I'll often urge them to do some deep breathing to help them calm down. I guide them through and breathe deeply with them. It's never failed to help my patients regain some of their composure.

> *Deep breathing is one of the best ways to lower stress in the body. This is because when you breathe deeply it sends a message to your brain to calm down and relax. The brain then sends this message to your body. Those things that happen when you are stressed, such as increased heart rate, fast breathing, and high blood pressure, all decrease as you breathe deeply to relax.* (Murray and Pizzorno, 2006)

Whenever I feel stressed, I make it a point to take at least ten deep breaths. I've learned to do it quietly so I can breathe deeply anywhere without drawing attention to myself. Oxygen fuels all our vital organs, reduces adrenaline in our bodies, and facilitates relaxation. I've sat through many meetings at work, breathing slowly and deeply, when I felt stressed or ill or both. I also use it when I'm weak from standing in lines at airports, post offices, and other locations where, without a wheelchair, sitting isn't an option. I find the focus on breathing keeps me calm as I wait. When I'm very sick, I try to breathe deeply for ten minutes every day. Unless you have a pulmonary disability, make a point to breathe slowly and deeply for a few minutes every day. You may be surprised how much better you feel.

Joanna J. Charnas, LICSW, LCSW

Wash Your Hands

Keeping your hands clean and away from your mouth, eyes, and nose is one of the easiest things you can do to avoid infection. It is prevention at its simplest and most fundamental. Remember to wash your hands whenever you return to your home or office and before you eat. With access to hand sanitizer, keeping your hands clean is even easier than it used to be. I keep a small bottle in my purse, my car, and on my desk at work. I am so susceptible to colds and the flu that I'm extremely careful about hand hygiene. It can't hurt, and many studies have proven it helps, so be conscientious about washing your hands in order to avoid infections.

Meditate Often

In 1998 I began meditating twice a day, and the practice improved my life dramatically (more on that in another chapter). I continue to meditate using a relaxation CD whenever I feel sick or stressed and still find its soothing effects beneficial. The Mayo Clinic's Website staff advises:

Meditation can give you a sense of calm, peace and balance that benefits both your emotional well-being and your overall health. And these benefits don't end when your meditation session ends. Meditation can help carry you more calmly through your day and can even improve certain medical conditions.[9]

There are many types of meditation, but perhaps the simplest and easiest way to explore meditation is to purchase a few meditation CDs in a health food store or online. Meditation CDs often use guided imagery or the progressive reduction of muscle tension to promote relaxation. The CDs customarily have narrators with soothing voices who lead you through the exercise. Try a few CDs until you find one that works for you. My meditation CD comes from the Benson-Henry Institute for Mind Body Medicine, which you can find online.[10] If you don't want to use CDs to meditate, you may search online for a website that outlines different methods. Even if meditating doesn't improve your health, if you practice it regularly, you may find yourself markedly less stressed as you manage your chronic illness.

Drink Enough Water

Drinking water is one of those great, easy, cheap things we can do for ourselves. Recently, someone said to me that water is to the human body as motor oil is to your car; it keeps everything running smoothly. Dr. Andrew Weil tells us "Water is a basic necessity, needed to maintain a healthy body, a clear mind, and a good balance within your tissues." He notes that water makes up about 60% of our bodies, and the supply constantly needs replenishing. He also recommends the standard eight 8-ounce glasses a day.[11]

I try to drink 1-2 liters of water a day. Some days, I manage to get down that much water. Often, I can't handle it if I'm out of the house frequently or in and out of meetings at work. I only advise drinking two liters (or eight glasses) of water daily if it's practical for you and if the benefits won't inconvenience you or disrupt other aspects of your life.

Sometimes, I think I have all this stuff under control and that I'm doing a great job taking care of myself, and then life throws me a curve ball. I once ran into trouble on an airplane when returning home to Boston after a week of visiting my brother and his family in San Francisco.

During the flight, I happily chugged water. I was adhering to my health regimen, which always feels good. Then, the plane hit turbulence that seemed to last a long time. The captain came on the public address system and told us he had ordered the flight attendants to sit down and put on their seat belts, implying the seriousness of the problem. The jostling awakened the baby one row behind me, and he began to howl. The plane bounced so much I couldn't keep the book I was reading at eye level. As I tried to read, my bladder felt increasingly full, and I quickly became uncomfortable.

The flight attendants finally were allowed to stand up, but they chastened any passenger who tried to do the same by stating, with cutting authority, "The seat belt sign is still on." The man sitting next to me stood up despite the lighted seatbelt sign and headed in the direction of the bathrooms. When my renegade seatmate returned, I weighed my options: urinating on myself in a public place with no chance of escape from embarrassment or risking life and limb with a run to the bathroom. I decided to take my chances on the latter, hoping the stewardesses would be too busy to reprimand me.

Once in the bathroom, I remembered a story I'd seen on television about a woman who hit her head and died during turbulence on a flight similar to mine. I thought, *Dear Lord, here I am with my pants around my ankles. This would be such an ignominious way to die!* But I managed to make it back to my seat without incident, even escaping notice by the flight attendants.

~

Simple things, like drinking enough water, shouldn't be so challenging, but sometimes they are. Living with chronic illness is all about making adjustments to the lives we once led. Sometimes the adjustments are easy, and occasionally things go completely haywire. We have to accept that we can't control everything and simply do our best day by day. Do whatever you can to support your general wellness. And whenever things don't go as smoothly as expected, laugh at yourself the way I did inside that airplane restroom!

Joanna J. Charnas, LICSW, LCSW

9

Learning to Juggle:
Orchestrating Your Life

Looks Can Be Deceiving

"Well . . . you *look* great!" Whenever people announce this when I'm ill, I bristle inside. I'd like to believe the speaker is attempting to be supportive, and what they meant to say is "You may be sick, but at least you're not looking bad." Often these comments feel dismissive, an implication that I can't possibly be sick because I don't appear wan and frail.

After an entire adulthood of poor health and over twenty-five years of social work, I've learned that feeling good and looking good don't necessarily correlate. Many sick people try hard to look as well as they can when they leave their homes to face the world. Most of us don't want attention for being sick. We work hard to be seen at our best, not our worst. Looking good is something tangible that makes us feel normal and encourages us as we work to maintain whatever good health we have, or, if we're fortunate, to return to the healthy lives we once enjoyed.

If someone says you look great when you're sick, you can respond in a variety of ways. If I think the speaker is well intentioned, I simply reply, "Thank you." But if I believe the person is being dismissive or doesn't understand I can be unwell without my illness being visible, I might add something like, "You can't see a hidden disability." You'll have to decide how *you* want to respond to people's comments on your appearance when you're sick. I always try to be polite, and I think of these encounters as opportunities to educate folks who might have little or no understanding of chronic illness.

How We Behave Is Not Always How We Feel

There is a significant difference between the purposeful presentation of a healthy life and a life free of the demands and limitations of illness. Many people with chronic illness *seem* to be normal. But our presentation in public does not always convey an accurate or complete picture. We struggle to present our healthiest selves to the world. Most of us don't want other people to see the down time, the planning required to function, and the moments of desperation, which take place primarily inside our homes.

People often interpret your ability to cope with or compensate for illness, or the simple act of hiding it, for actual good health. The better you cope, the less likely others may be to accept that you are genuinely ill. I remember a conversation I once had with a well-intentioned co-worker. Although she knew I had Chronic Fatigue Syndrome and had been sick recently, she commented that I seemed energetic. I told her the reason she believed I had a lot of energy *all the time* was because she only observed me when I felt energized. I explained to her that when I wasn't well, I made a point to remain in my office, quietly taking care of business. She didn't see this side of me at work not because it didn't exist, but because I went out of my way to conceal it from her and my other colleagues.

I once worked with a woman who had severe rheumatoid arthritis. Despite her condition, she led a busy, active life. She confided in me that people often asked how she could stay so busy, as if they questioned the fact that she had a serious and painful condition. My colleague explained remaining active was how she coped with her arthritis and kept her mind off the pain. Unfortunately, the very aspect of her life that helped her cope with illness also sometimes made people question its existence.

CREATING BALANCE

My life is a constant balancing act of trying to nourish my mind, body, and soul, holding down a full time job, and maintaining numerous relationships with friends, family, and romantic partners. I realize the balancing act I strive for isn't just a challenge for people living with chronic illness; it is the hue and cry of every working woman I know. However, living with chronic illness increases those challenges. Sometimes my body's needs require so much stamina, my whole ecosystem is thrown off balance. Since my relapse in 1996, illness has forced me to re-evaluate constantly how I conduct my daily life in ways I never had to previously. I'm always trying to get the balance of needs in better sync. This is a lofty goal because, while my intellectual, emotional, and spiritual needs remain fairly constant, my physical needs often vary greatly from day to day, and even from hour to hour. I've learned to live with a tremendous amount of unpredictability. I accept this unpredictability as normal for me, and it no longer causes me despair as it once did.

I view every day as an adventure. Sometimes the adventure goes way off course, and I must be present to the moment's demands and figure out how to make it to the next moment. My patients have also told me that sometimes the adage "one day at a time" can be too much to handle. I advise them to break an overwhelming day into segments. I encourage them to focus on the next meal, for example. Or if they're really having a tough time, I help them focus on the next hour. When life's an adventure because of physical or mental illness, we can break up the day into manageable blocks of time. This philosophy helps me survive my bad days, and my patients respond positively to the concept.

You will want to learn, over time, how to create your own balance and to make peace with it on your own terms. It's achievable, and you can learn to be happy living within its parameters once you've adjusted to the demands of your illness.

Spend Some Money!

In addition to advice about guilt, my mother also said, "There's no problem so big it won't get at least a little better if you throw some money at it." I have found this to be true over and over again. I know money is in short supply for many who live with illness. Often people are on fixed incomes that severely limit their financial flexibility. I understand throwing money at a problem is not possible for everyone. But when it's an option, it's worth considering.

In the late 1990's, I had an episode of extreme fatigue combined with severe sinus problems. I was home for two weeks, the end of which was usually the point in time when I became desperate and frantic. Medical science was doing nothing to help me. My father told me he'd heard acupuncture could be an effective treatment for sinus problems and suggested I see an acupuncturist. Unfortunately,

I didn't think I had the extra cash for out-of-pocket care until I remembered the "Zoe goes to college fund."

Years before, when I first adopted my cat, Zoe, I'd tried unsuccessfully to buy health insurance for her. Instead, I began to save twenty-five dollars a month for Zoe's health care. I jokingly called my cache the "Zoe Goes to College Fund." When Zoe's "college" fund reached a thousand dollars, I stopped contributing.

That fall, I decided to spend the money I'd saved for Zoe. She was perfectly healthy, whereas I was desperate and sick. It was an easy decision. I took my father's suggestion and saw an acupuncturist the first day I felt well enough to leave the house. I continued appointments with him for a couple of months. I had no idea whether or not his treatments were helping me, but I found them surprisingly relaxing, which kept me returning. I stopped seeing the acupuncturist when Zoe's fund reached two hundred dollars. I'd moved out of the worst of the relapse by then.

I spent Zoe's college fund because I needed help right away. Zoe was less than ten years old when I dipped into her savings, so I had plenty of time to rebuild her medical fund. Throwing some money at my problem helped me physically and made me feel more empowered because I was being proactive. Mom would have been proud.

LEARN TO PRIORITIZE

It's important to prioritize how you expend energy when illness limits it. I have a motto: *Movies First.* If I had a family, my motto would be *Family First.* I love movies and prefer to see them in a movie theater. I've gone to the movies at least once a week for forty years. Among my friends and family, I'm often known as the person who "sees everything." When I have the time and the energy, the first thing I do is go to the movies. I'm often at the earliest of the early bird matinees on Saturday mornings. I stagger into the theater at 10:40 for the 10:45 show, along with other film fanatics. But when I go to the movies on Saturday morning, I know whatever else happens during the weekend, I've made time for the part of my life I care about the most. Sometimes my home isn't as clean as it needs to be, and then I can look forward to watching the dust bunnies drift across my floor. But because my health is so unpredictable, it's essential to prioritize my activities. Monday through Friday, my priority is work. On the weekend, it's getting to the movies.

Often it isn't possible for me to do everything I need to in order to keep my life on track the way I want. I have to let go of certain things. Prioritize what you care about most, and give those matters your time and energy first. Let go of what is less important to you. Eventually the less important things get done anyway. I pay my bills, and, sooner or later, I clean the house. When I look at the big picture, everything works out, and it can work for you too.

~

I am the master of my own three-ring circus, keeping health in the center ring. Sometimes, the show goes off without a hitch, but occasionally there is pandemonium. As the ringmaster, I plan well, balance the components of my life carefully, and remain optimistic. These are the best ways I've successfully managed a complex life with chronic illness.

10

Overwhelmed?
Create a Backup System

Even though I was sick, I look back fondly on what I refer to as my Francis Ford Film Festival. That day I watched, in sequence, all three *Godfather* movies directed by the great Francis Ford Coppola. I viewed them through my cat Libby's ears, which framed the TV as she sat at the foot of my bed. I'd taped the movies earlier and saved them for a day when I needed to rest. I'd seen each of the *Godfather* films when they first came out but had never watched them all at once before. Resting with Libby and distracting myself with this great cinematic saga provided me with relief on a day when I was ill and uncomfortable

Creating back-up systems to help you accomplish the essential tasks of living and to take care of yourself when you're sick is important if you're living with chronic illness. Following are some areas in which to consider establishing back-up systems, as well as examples of the systems I've created for myself.

EAT WELL WHEN YOU'RE SICK

Good nutrition is important to us at all times, and it becomes even more critical when we're very sick. If you're too sick to prepare food, you don't want to sustain yourself solely on home delivered pizza, as enticing as this may seem. If you like to cook, you might try preparing food in quantity and keeping your freezer stocked with meals that only need defrosting and heating. I *don't like to cook*, except in my crockpot. I make large amounts of my favorite dishes in the crockpot and freeze the resulting half-dozen meals. I don't even like to cook pasta, but I'll prepare rice pasta and freeze it in meal-size portions for one. Then, when I'm sick, I quickly defrost the pasta in the microwave, add ingredients I have on hand to add nutritional value and flavor, and *voilà*, dinner is served!

Explore commercial frozen and canned foods you might like, and keep your home well stocked with them if, like me, you don't like to cook or aren't well enough to do so. I am a sucker for all things Trader Joe's. A week's worth of their frozen dinners is always available in my freezer.

Take-out food is another option to consider if you have the financial resources. Even the most rural areas of the country often have one or two restaurants. If they don't usually offer take-out, they might be willing to provide it for you if you establish a relationship with the restaurant's management. For those of us who live in more urban environments, there are usually hosts of take-out options, many of which may be delivered to our door. When you're so sick that brushing your teeth seems like a daunting task, you'll be glad on your healthier days you prepared to eat well despite the circumstances.

GET YOUR LAUNDRY DONE

Washing clothes and linens is another essential life task that can seem overwhelming when you're not feeling well. The physical labor required for this job can be exhausting. I've sometimes made myself much sicker by doing my laundry. I thought I was up to it and realized later, after washing, drying, folding, and putting it away, that I'd miscalculated. Before I moved into my condo with a washer and dryer less than eight feet from my bedroom, I made it a point to own a three-week supply of underwear so I could always have clean underpants on hand if I didn't feel well enough to run a load of wash. In the past, when I was very sick, I used a commercial laundry and paid them to heave the clothes in and out of machines and fold them.

I once knew a woman, also with Chronic Fatigue Syndrome, who had a special arrangement with a friend. He would help with laundry and, in exchange, she would buy him dinner. She lived several flights up in a building with no elevator and didn't have the physical stamina to carry her laundry up and down the stairs. Her friend was happy to help her, and she was glad to thank him by treating him to a meal.

ARRANGE FOR TRANSPORTATION

For a long time, my former husband, Harry, used the family car to commute to work, and I took public transportation to my job. I tried to keep cab fare in my house in case I had a medical emergency. Once, though, I nearly passed out as I was about to board the elevator to go home from work on a Friday night. I suddenly became so lightheaded, it caught me completely off guard and took me a minute to figure out what I needed to do. When I recovered from my shock, I turned around, went into my supervisor's office, and told her what was happening. She made me lie on her floor and drink some water. When I felt a little better, she walked me to a cab. I came very close to passing out in the cab, but I made it home without fainting and felt better in a few hours. After that experience, I carried emergency cab fare with me at all times until I began commuting to work by car.

ENTERTAIN YOURSELF

Sometimes, I'm so sick I can't do much of anything. I spend most of my time between meals sleeping. Other times, I may be sick but have enough energy to read or watch television. Consequently, I'm in the habit of recording interesting television programs and saving them for when I'm ill. I watched the PBS Ken Burns' mini-series, *The Civil War,* this way, as well as many other engrossing mini-series and movies. I also keep a small stack of unread books in the house at all times. I have an assortment of easy reading as well as material that is more challenging. During one relapse, I read four great bestsellers over eight days. So physically fatigued I could barely move, I still had enough mental energy to read, and that made feeling ill and being stuck at home much easier. Books and recorded television programs have helped distract me, reduce stress, and promote physical healing.

HOME MAKING

Recently a colleague referred me to Care.com.[12] This organization provides many homemaking services on an emergency basis, such as housecleaning, cooking, and child and pet care. My friends speak highly of this service, and there may be agencies in your community that will provide, for a fee, similar emergency assistance.

~

Back-up systems mitigate some of the stress when illness overwhelms us. They help us continue to run our lives smoothly and make it through the day. With good back-up systems in place, we can weather setbacks more easily and return to our baseline sooner than later.

Joanna J. Charnas, LICSW, LCSW

11

Relationships:
What Did You Just Say? Dealing
with Friends, Family, and Others

I'd been working at the hospital for over a year and began to feel as though I was living a secret double life: Competent Clinical Social Worker by day, treating patients on the psychiatry wards, and clandestine sick person at home struggling to take care of myself. Feeling sad that I couldn't be open and authentic with anyone at work about the full scope of my life, I realized there was one person I'd overlooked. My mentor and I had spent a year building a trusting and warm relationship, so I decided to "come out" to her about my illness. When I disclosed my health issues to her, she responded with kindness and understanding. To this day, she continues to encourage me to take care of myself, even if it means missing work. After telling my mentor I had Chronic Fatigue Syndrome, I was pleased I'd taken a leap of faith and broken my isolation at work by sharing this part of my life with her.

Dealing with the people in our lives is one of the most challenging aspects of living with chronic illness. They may be compassionate and understanding or completely insensitive. Below are some of the interpersonal issues we face now that illness affects our lives.

UNDERSTANDING THE PERIOD OF ADJUSTMENT

When you become ill, you aren't the only person going through a period of adjustment to your new life. Your friends and family are almost certainly also going through their own periods of adjustment. They may be mourning your losses and/or be worried about your new challenges, just as you are.

Don't assume the people in your life are able to discuss their feelings about your illness with you. All of us struggle to understand our emotions at some point in our lives. Your loved ones may need time to sort out how they feel. In addition, they might struggle with expressing those feelings to you. Sometimes, the feelings emerge as anger or grief, common reactions. Human beings are flawed, and the most well intentioned of us don't always say the right thing all of the time. It's reasonable to ask for compassion, but then be flexible with your loved ones. Remember, if you're in a process, so are they.

Frequently, the people in your life will be at least one step behind you as you navigate a new life with chronic illness. Although it can be challenging, try to be patient with your loved ones if you find them falling short of how you hoped they would behave. Give them time.

Sometimes, others will express their compassion in exactly the right way. Early in my marriage my husband, Harry, and I went to my mother-in-law's home for dinner. I was feeling sick, but she'd cooked an elaborate four-course meal for us, and I didn't want to disappoint her by canceling. Before dinner, I lay on her couch as we all chatted. When my mother-in-law left the room briefly, I reached out my hand behind me toward Harry. Without a word, he grasped my hand and held it quietly until his mother re-entered the room. In those moments, I felt his complete support and understanding. This is one of the warmest memories from my marriage.

REACTING TO OTHERS

As scared as you may be by your new life with chronic illness, it's fair to assume that at least some of the people in your life are also scared for you. They may react to your illness by being available to you emotionally. Others might be available to you for practical help, such as assisting with household chores or providing food. Some people may completely shut down on you, too scared to deal with your illness at all. Others will only show an interest in your health when they think you're making poor decisions, even though they were never involved or supportive of your good ones. If you had a full social life with friends, family, and colleagues before you became sick, you'll probably encounter all these reactions.

It's beneficial to decide how you want to respond to each person in your life. How you deal with a co-worker may not be the same as how you react to your mother-in-law. My situation is complicated because I have an illness not yet fully understood by the medical establishment and is often misjudged. I think I've improved my responses when people are hurtful, but I'm still surprised every time it happens. For example, sometimes people imply that my illness isn't real by pointing out that there's no diagnostic test for Chronic Fatigue Syndrome. When this happens, I quietly explain that diagnosing CFS is done by ruling out all other physical and psychiatric illnesses, the same way

Alzheimer's disease is diagnosed. No one doubts Alzheimer's is a real disease. Once I've discussed Alzheimer's with skeptics, they're more open to accepting that Chronic Fatigue Syndrome is also real.

You may want to give some thought to how you will deal with well-intentioned as well as insensitive people when they say hurtful things. My friend, Amy, who has two chronic illnesses, says that learning to effectively communicate information about your illness takes practice, as does any skill, such as playing a musical instrument. Over time, you can refine this particular skill until you're able to respond graciously when caught off guard or when someone has accidentally hurt your feelings. Every circumstance is different, and as long as you remain sick, you'll always have opportunities to develop this skill.

MANAGING CONTROL ISSUES

Even though it may not seem this way, when you're sick, you're the only person in control. This can be extremely frustrating for your loved ones. As out of control as you may feel because of your illness, the people in your life may feel even *more* out of control. At least you have some sense of what your needs are. You're experiencing being sick while they're experiencing it only vicariously and are trying to figure out how to respond. In most cases, you'll be armed with far more information than they are.

Anyone who's had a person close to them go through an illness knows there's a great feeling of helplessness that occurs during this experience. My mother died when she was forty-nine years old, and I watched her health decline for years before she passed away. I made numerous suggestions as well as offers of help, but she rejected almost all of them. I could do nothing as I watched her become increasingly disabled. The truth is, while dying at forty-nine is tragic, my mother's life was her own, not mine. I had to come to terms with the reality that she was in control of her health, and nothing I said or did would change that.

Our loved ones don't want us to be sick. Often, the behaviors they exhibit are attempts to regain some of the control they feel they've lost. Their words and actions may be helpful, but sometimes they're not. For example, if you're too sick to describe your symptoms to your doctor, then it's helpful if a friend, family member, neighbor, or the person you live with insists on accompanying you to your medical appointment. Conversely, if that person is going with you to the doctor because she wants to control the outcome of the visit, then it's intrusive and inappropriate.

DIFFERENT KINDS OF SUPPORT

People will support us in vastly different ways. Try to be open to the different kinds of help offered. For example, my brother, Charles, is supportive in numerous ways, large and small, in many areas of my life. His support includes encouraging me to exercise. Over the years, he's bought me a workout bag, walking and running shoes, and gave me his swimming goggles. If I have an exercise routine, he'll ask me how it's going. If I'm not exercising regularly, he'll encourage me to begin. He never pushes me to exercise more than I can manage or tries to dictate the kind of exercise I choose. He simply helps keep exercise in the forefront of my mind.

When I'm sick, it's easy to let things slide in my life, but it's important to prioritize exercising when I have the necessary strength. Charles understands this about me and is supportive by helping me make the right choice. He doesn't say, "I love you and I'm worried about you because you're sick." Yet, I know that Charles' reminders to exercise are one of the ways he shows he cares. They are expressions of concern and love, and I'm grateful for them.

SHARING INFORMATION

It's helpful to figure out how much about your illness you want to share with the people in your life. We all have our own communication styles. Mine is to verbalize everything. I recognize that my style can be overwhelming, so I'm always conscience of how much I talk about my health. I know people care, but they don't want to hear about it all the time. Many of my friends and family members routinely ask me how I'm feeling, and I respond briefly. I try to avoid allowing my health to take center stage in any conversation unless I'm very sick and it's the focus of my life at that time. You can decide how much you want to share about your health with the people in your life, and how much they want to hear. It serves our relationships well to be mindful of how much we talk about our health.

SHARING WITH PARTNERS

How much you tell your partner about your health from day to day is an especially delicate matter. It depends on how sick you are, how involved your partner is in your care, how much you need to involve him, and how much he needs to hear. Here are some important issues to consider:

- How much do you need to tell your partner about your health in order to feel cared for?

- How much does your partner want to hear?

- What is overwhelming for her to hear, or for you to talk about?

- Does your partner want to know more than you want to share?

- How does giving or withholding information about your health affect your relationship?

- What meaning does sharing or withholding have for you?

- Does your partner's attentiveness to your illness make you feel cared for, or does it make you feel as though you have to report to him?

- Does telling your partner how you feel make her feel dumped on?

- What's going to work for the relationship, not just for the individuals?

PARTNERS IN GENERAL

Some of us have partners who understand our illnesses and are involved in our care. Other partners are not involved in our care but are compassionate and understanding. Still other people have partners who are caring but are unable to become significantly involved in the day-to-day struggles of our illness, whether the struggles are practical or emotional.

If your partner is caring and wants to help in whatever way he can, you're fortunate despite your illness. Often, issues involving our partners and our health are neither black nor white but some shade of gray. Most of our partners are neither saintly nor completely insensitive. Sometimes they are going to be kind and caring, and sometimes, they are going to be distracted, disinterested, or brusque. We need to explore and define our feelings about how our partners react to our needs. For example, I had an HIV-positive client whose relationship with his partner began when he was robust and fully functional. The client ran his own business and was vigorous and active. When my client became symptomatic, his partner was resentful and didn't seem to understand or accept the changes in my client's daily capabilities. The partner belittled the client for attending an HIV support group. However, he also insisted on accompanying my client to his doctor's appointments and would remind him to take his medications on time. This partner, neither all good nor all bad, was clearly scared and conflicted. Although saddened by the lack of support he sometimes felt, my client didn't vilify him. Instead, he simply stood firm in taking care of his health interests even when his partner discouraged him.

Try to avoid making your partner "wrong." It will help immensely to accept your partner's limitations. Do your best to make your relationship work within those boundaries. However, if you're badly in need of help and your partner behaves as if nothing has changed or is unwilling to provide assistance, consider what is keeping you bound to this person. If you cannot meet your basic needs, your partner has some moral obligation to help. If she refuses, that is neglect. You shouldn't accept such a situation, and you will need to find a way to change your relationship. You might want to attend couple's counseling to address your issues and explore solutions. As a last resort, you might need to end your relationship if the neglect continues. We sometimes face these painful matters after we become ill. There are no easy answers to such relationship issues except to be thoughtful about our decisions.

On the other hand, some of us have partners who become overly involved. They try to do everything for us whether we need it or not. This can make us feel more dependent or sicker than we actually are. If you have an overly involved partner, try to find a way to let him know he's making you feel worse, not better. Gently asking him to step back and reassuring him you can manage for yourself may be effective.

Some partners, in an effort to regain lost control, involve themselves too much in our medical decisions. If this happens to you, the most important thing to remember in matters concerning your body is that *you* should be making the final decisions. As long as you are mentally competent, you have the right to be in charge. Never let anyone take this right away from you. Your partner may serve as a fine sounding board or have valuable ideas or a helpful perspective. You may choose to consider her opinions, but you should make the final decisions. Remember, it's your health, your body, and ultimately your life.

ASKING FOR UNDERSTANDING

You deserve to have people in your life who understand the challenges of living with illness and who accept you as you are. We don't need others to judge us. Each of us needs friends and family who respect the way we choose to and need to live. They must accept our limitations as well as the choices we make in order to remain as healthy as possible.

My friend, James, has Meniere's Syndrome, an inner ear disorder. I once saw him at a party during a weekend he'd planned to vacation in New Orleans. When I spotted him, I asked him why he wasn't with his friend in Louisiana. James, who is completely deaf in one ear, a result of his illness, explained he had an infection in his good ear and couldn't afford to risk damaging it by flying. When I inquired how his friend felt about the canceled trip, his reply was matter of fact.

"Well, he's my friend, so he understands."

Everything this statement implied impressed me. Each of us living with chronic illness is entitled to this kind of acceptance and understanding.

Another friend of mine, Grace, has multiple sclerosis. Before I moved from Boston to California, she was my number one movie buddy, and we frequently went to the movies together. She and I have an unspoken understanding: If one of us needs to rest or go home, we stop whatever we're doing. We never complain if our plans have to change suddenly. I don't expect the same innate understanding from my healthy friends, but I do expect acceptance, and the more I expect, the more I receive. It's all right to ask for the compassion and understanding you need. You deserve it.

TRUST YOURSELF

You should trust that you know yourself better than anyone else does. You may have a hard-to-diagnose illness or one about which little is known by the medical community. You might have spent hundreds of hours researching your illness on the Internet or elsewhere and be better informed about it than your doctor is. And you certainly know more about your symptoms than anyone else does. Never let anyone—friends, family, partner, or doctor, whether well intentioned or not—persuade you otherwise.

ASKING FOR HELP

Asking for help is a tricky and sometimes difficult matter. Most of us want to remain as independent as possible, so sometimes we refuse help when it's offered or don't ask for help when we should. Asking for help means accepting our own limitations, which is often painful. In the past, I've made myself sicker in an effort to pull my load or take care of myself. Now I think in terms of balance. I try to determine what I can physically manage and weigh it with what asking for help will cost me emotionally.

Figure out when you genuinely need help, and don't make yourself sicker because you're afraid to ask for it. But also try to be honest. Don't ask for assistance unless you need it because ultimately your independence serves you well and will make you feel better about your life.

~

We humans are innately social creatures, and our nature includes flaws. Everything is a learning process for us as well as for the people in our lives. We're learning how to take care of ourselves and how to interact with others within the imposed confines of our illness, and our loved ones are responding the best way they can. Be patient and forgiving. Don't remain stuck in a negative emotion because someone hurts your feelings or you didn't get what you needed from them. Be grateful when people are kind and caring, and let go of everything else. You'll have a happier life if you do.

Joanna J. Charnas, LICSW, LCSW

12

I Want You. I Love You. I'm Sick.

How Do I Tell You I'm Sick?

Even the most self-confident person dislikes rejection when dating. It doesn't feel good. We put our best selves forward and hope the person in front of us will see our strengths and charms. Sometimes they do, and sometimes they don't. Most of the time when they don't, it's not personal. Our date simply wants a quality we can't offer, but when chronic illness complicates our lives, this added element may make us feel insecure.

I was diagnosed with Chronic Fatigue Syndrome during my marriage. Prior to receiving this news, I had nothing to disclose. I wasn't well much of the time, but I didn't feel the need to discuss that part of my life early in a relationship. After my divorce, with the knowledge of my health condition, I felt an ethical obligation to inform potential partners about this aspect of my life.

I choose to tell love interests about my illness as soon as we begin to develop a level of emotional or physical intimacy. Usually this happens around the third date. This is a good strategy for me. Since my divorce in 2001, I've told almost a dozen men about my illness while getting to know them. No one has run for the hills.

I've gradually pared down my disclosure to a few sentences. At this point, I could set it to music and tap dance as I tell a potential significant other: *I've had CFS since I was nineteen. I've always led a full life, including work and relationships. I don't expect anyone to take care of me, but I do need to rest a lot.* That's all I say.

When you disclose your illness, be straightforward and honest. This isn't the time to be emotional. Sharing your deepest feelings about your illness with your new partner may be fine, but the moment you first mention your situation isn't the right time for that. You want to minimize the drama and pain of your illness at this moment so you and your date can have a calm conversation about it. Answer any questions he may have, but save the discussion of your deeper emotions for when you're more involved later in the relationship and you've developed trust with each other. Failing to inform a potential partner about this part of your life may have negative repercussions in the future and might feel like a lie of omission to your partner. If you tell you too much, though, you run the risk of overwhelming her. So, keep your disclosure clear and brief.

If someone rejects you because of your illness, be grateful. It's good when a prospective partner knows her limitations. It's okay for her to say she isn't able to date someone with illness. Don't make her wrong for this. She's saved you heartbreak in the future by being honest with you now. Although it may seem unfair, it's the nature of all dating.

When we date, we need to determine for ourselves what we want and who will meet our needs. I can't date men who are extremely athletic and looking for a partner to join them in their athletic activities. I don't have the stamina for anything but long walks and even then only when I'm well. It's a deal breaker for me. Sometimes, children or animals are the deal breakers. People don't want the encumbrances of a partner who's responsible for living beings. or they don't want the potential problems that might accompany shared child rearing with an ex-spouse. One of my friends won't date smokers. We all have things we can and cannot accept in relationships. So, if someone needs a healthier partner, accept his preferences and limitations and move on. You're seeking the right person, not a fantasy.

If you have a physical disability that's visible or significantly limiting and you're going on a blind date, tell your date upfront about your appearance or limitations before planning a get-together. People have a right to make informed decisions. Once, I'd been e-mailing and talking to a man I met on an Internet dating website. We agreed to meet for coffee, but as I was about to hang up the phone, he casually informed me that his arms were very short due to a birth defect. I felt duped but decided to go on the date and see how it evolved. His arms were about half the normal length, and his hands were also misshapen. I spent two hours getting to know this man and decided not to date him again for other reasons, but I thought springing his birth defect on me when he did put me in an awkward position. I met another man on the Internet who told me he had a prosthetic leg. Early in our dialogue, he mentioned his leg and the illness that necessitated amputation. I respected him for sharing this part of his life when he did.

Don't assume you know how people will respond to your disclosure. Information resonates differently with each person and situation. I once had a brief, intense relationship with a man named Pete. On our third date, I told him I had CFS. At some unmemorable moment later in our relationship, I mentioned I'd had a pre-cancerous mole removed the summer before. (The mole removal resulted in two outpatient procedures, each requiring stitches and a total of four weeks of wound care, leaving me with a two-inch scar on my buttocks. I like to say I literally have a big-ass scar. However, I didn't share any of these details with Pete.)

Pete seemed completely unconcerned with my CFS, but several times during our relationship, he mentioned my pre-cancerous mole and his worry about my getting cancer in the future. This experience reminded me not to assume how a potential partner will react when I tell him I have a chronic illness and to let him experience the information in his own way.

Despite the media's proclivity for portraying a standard template of what's attractive, the truth is that most of us date and have long-term, intimate relationships. People with chronic illness, terminal illness, morbid obesity, amputations, and paraplegia all date, fall in love, cohabitate, and marry. We *all* have the potential to be the love of someone's life, regardless of our health or the state of our bodies. Attraction is a deeply personal matter. At best, it's flexible. Someone might find her partner attractive at a healthy weight as well as after he's gained fifty pounds. At worst, it's rigid, and our partners only desire us when our appearance and lives are the same as when we first met. Our best option is to be open with the people we date. If they reject us due to our illness, we can move on until we find someone who will love us and accept us for the totality of who we are.

SEX!

Being touched is inherently good for us. We live longer, and touch boosts our immune system. Much research supports these facts. I particularly liked the March 2014 online article at Exhibit Health[13] that describes the science of touch. Sex is also good for us. It releases an influx of happy hormones into our system, including dopamine, serotonin, oxytocin, and vasopressin. Helen Fisher's seminal book, *The Anatomy of Love: A Natural History of Mating, Marriage, and Why We Stray* (1994), details this phenomenon.

Sex can be scary, though, if you have physical limitations. It's easy to worry you'll be rejected if you don't present yourself like a supermodel or star athlete. However, the components of a healthy and satisfying sex life are the same whether we're ill, disabled, or neither: honesty, trust, respect, and good communication.

In 2011, two remarkably similar movies were released: *No Strings Attached* and *Friends with Benefits*. Both films depict young couples in their late twenties to early thirties attempting sexual relationships without emotional attachments. Because these were Hollywood products, the couples in the films fall in love and become committed romantic partners, but what struck me about these movies were the frank sexual negotiations each couple engaged in prior to having sex. I thought how great it might be to talk to my next partner this openly about sex *before* we became intimate.

Shortly after the second film's release, I met someone. When he sensed our relationship would include physical intimacy, he asked me a string of explicit and direct questions about my preferences in bed. This felt like magical wish fulfillment. The conversation didn't decrease the romance or excitement of our relationship. We developed a happy sex life from the baseline knowledge we initially discussed. An open conversation about your likes and dislikes, including your limitations, can be the groundwork for great sex.

If your chronic illness affects your energy, causes you pain, decreases your libido, or impacts your emotional equilibrium on a regular basis, a focused conversation with your partner or prospective partner may be helpful. For example, you might have a partner who prefers morning sex, but you find yourself waking up stiff or in pain because of a new medical issue. The best way to manage this change is through communication and compromise. Perhaps you prefer to wait to take your pain medication at noon so it will last until bedtime. Your compromise might be to occasionally take the medication in the morning. (Always check with your doctor prior to changing your medication regimen.) You can explore your partner's preference for sex in the morning and see if there are ways to bring those elements into the evening. If she's tired at night, help her with daily chores so she can conserve energy for sex. Work to find effective compromises so you retain the sizzle and emotional satisfaction of this part of your lives.

If the sex you're accustomed to is no longer physically comfortable because of anatomical changes or pain, consider buying a copy of *The Joy of Sex: The Ultimate Revised Edition* by Alex Comfort (2009). This contemporary version of the original book, published in 1972, continues to be a dependable go-to resource. The book might help you explore new positions and information to accommodate your current capabilities and needs.

No matter what resources and approaches we implement, sometimes our illnesses *do* affect our romantic lives. We need to be flexible and request the same from our partners, but even when we're not well, we can make an effort to put our best foot forward. Several years ago, I canceled a date to go dancing with a boyfriend because I was too ill to get off the couch. I asked him if we could hang out at my house instead. He agreed, and when he arrived for the evening, he found me dressed in the cutest, sexiest loungewear I owned. I didn't greet him at the door wearing sweats. I'd recorded hours of one of his favorite television shows, and I offered to watch this show with him instead of choosing a pay-per-view movie together. I gave him the best I had to offer at that moment, and we had a lovely, warm evening together.

When you're chronically ill and in a relationship, you can still make an effort to give your best to a partner even when you don't feel well. Conversely, if you have a partner whose needs you understand but whose illness is now impacting your sex life, focus on maximizing the positive. Do what works. *The Waterdance,* a wonderful independent movie released in 1992, depicts an accident victim as he recovers and adjusts to paraplegia. The movie shows the protagonist and other patients in rehab attending a class on sex, which includes a discussion about their inability to have intercourse and their new focus on oral sex. Later in the movie, we hear the lead character and his girlfriend loudly having sex behind a curtain. We know he's doing what works. You might also include adult toys in your sex life if you want to spice things up or have a broader range of options at your disposal.

It's so easy to focus on our losses instead of our strengths. Talk to your new or current partner about what you *can* do to meet both your needs. Any sex that is consensual and includes discussion of safe practices is available to you. Be adventurous and open, and you may discover new ways to sexually satisfy each other. An eager, open partner can be extremely sexy.

~

The losses we experience with illness are challenging, but we need to demystify sex and think of our ability to have a gratifying sex life as just another of those challenges. Learning to maintain or create a satisfying sex life when you live with illness is a process; accept that there may be speed bumps along the way. Pay attention to your partner's needs and preferences. Be mindful, honest, and giving, and you can continue to have a satisfying, happy sex life.

13

Have Fun!
Cut Your Own Hair,
and Beets are Awesome

HAVING FUN

The great Shakespearean actor, Morris Carnovsky (1897-1992), thrust his fist into the air, forcefully pulled it toward his chest as if ringing a heavy bell, and bellowed to my class in his best King Lear voice, "You have to squeeze the orange!" The nineteen and twenty-year-old students in class that day understood his point: to make the most of what life offers. Thirty-two years later at our first reunion, many of my classmates remembered Morris's advice. I've quoted him throughout my life, and I use his lesson as one of my guiding principles.

When you live with illness, fun often takes a back seat to simply remaining functional, but the people I know who are the most successful at living with chronic illness are the ones who know how to have fun despite their conditions. Part of their success is that they've learned how to enjoy unexpected experiences. Now that illness has altered our circumstances, it helps to learn how to squeeze the orange in new and creative ways so we can continue to have fun in our lives.

A blind date once confided in me that he wanted to have more fun. I replied that fun was a driving force in my life. He asked how I achieved this. His question caught me off guard, and I had to think for some time before I could respond. I finally said that to have fun, I merged the best parts of myself with the best aspects of any situation. It's a simple concept, but in order to embody it, I have to be open and ready.

We can have fun doing almost anything. This may take us by surprise. One year, I stayed home for about two weeks because of illness. I remained flat on my back for the first week. By the beginning of the second week, I realized I badly needed a haircut. I couldn't stand looking at my shaggy head anymore. My former hairdresser had disappeared, I didn't know how to reach him, and I had no idea where to get a decent haircut.

I called a salon for which I had a discount coupon and asked for a stylist adept at cutting curly hair. Even though I felt lousy, two days later I dragged myself to the salon and waited my turn for the desired stylist, who didn't take appointments. When I met her, I explained that I wanted my shoulder-length hair layered from the top down.

I usually don't have my hair blown dry after a cut, so I go home with a damp head. I didn't realize until I returned to my apartment that I had "helmet head" down to my ears, like Alfalfa from *The Little Rascals*, minus the cowlick. Much too sick to go out again to have my helmet head fixed, I just sat around fuming.

I didn't want to spend the day upset about my hair, so I decided to take matters into my own hands. I'd cut my bangs before and had seen my hair cut innumerable times. How hard could it be to give myself a small trim? Intending only to give myself a little snip here and there, I soon found myself in the midst of a cutting frenzy. Brown curls littered my bathroom floor. To my surprise, the more I cut, the happier I felt. Before I knew it, I was experiencing a hair-styling high even though I had no idea what I was doing. At some point, I forced myself to stop, but I'd had more fun than I'd ever thought possible. For years afterward, I enjoyed a small contact high every time I remembered this experience.

When my husband returned home that afternoon, I asked him what he thought of my hairdo. Harry said it looked good, and I proudly blurted out that I'd cut much of it myself. He was impressed, and my confidence swelled further. Later that evening, after evaluating my work in front of a mirror, I decided I needed to do a little more cleaning up. I found myself grooving on the same self-styling high all over again.

The lesson I learned from my hair-cutting foray is that I don't have to be well to enjoy life. I can have fun doing anything at any time. The attitude and openness I bring to my existence determines whether I enjoy it, and my illness only dictates my happiness if I let it. Don't fall into the trap of thinking you can only have fun when you're feeling well. Be open to fun at all times. And remember, life is still our oyster, whether we're sick or not.

BEETS ARE AWESOME: ENJOYING THE LITTLE THINGS

I didn't enjoy beets until my early fifties, but after one divine beet-and goat-cheese salad in New Mexico, I became a fan. As luck would have it, beets are a staple of the cafeteria salad bar at the Naval Hospital where I work. One day, when the salad bar was out of beets, I asked a cafeteria worker if someone could bring more from the kitchen. I told her I'd just developed a taste for them and had been looking forward to eating beets on my salad.

"Oh yes", she replied with more enthusiasm than expected. "Beets are awesome!"

Really? Beets? I was surprised and impressed by the amount of positivity she'd brought to our conversation. I wanted that kind of enthusiasm for something as mundane as a root vegetable.

On the psychiatry wards at work, we often ask suicidal patients to write lists of "reasons to live." If I compiled this list for myself, on the top of it would be my morning cup of coffee. I find it deeply satisfying. I can count on it to make every day more pleasurable. On weekends when I go to a very early matinee, I forego my cup of coffee until later in the day in order to avoid needing to use the bathroom during the show. When this happens, I miss it badly.

One of my former bosses and a great psychiatrist, Dr. Saure, once informed me that studies have proven people live longer when they enjoy the little things in life. When chronic illness affects us, our days may become severely restricted. Our ability to embrace life's small pleasures is important if we want to maximize quality of life. On my worst days, I enjoy that first cup of coffee, the smell of good soap, the peace of my home, the soft fur of my cats, clean pretty lounge clothes, and the avocado plant I'm nurturing on my patio. I love all of these things, even at my sickest. One of my grandmothers lived to be one hundred years old. If I continue to embrace the simple pleasures of my life, I might live to be that old, too!

My patients tell me cafeteria duty is one of the worst assignments you can have, but I'll always be grateful for the girl with the big smile, great attitude, and love of beets who reminded me of an important life lesson. She was so right: beets *are* awesome, if you're willing to think of them that way.

~

When bad health gives you the blues, try to remember the small things in life that provide pleasure. Embrace them. Figure out ways you can infuse some fun into your day. Be creative, take control, and focus on the positive. This will help you enjoy life whether you're feeling your best or not.

Joanna J. Charnas, LICSW, LCSW

14

Exploring Complementary Care

I'm reluctant to admit this, but I started studying Tae Kwon Do because a psychic I knew and trusted told me learning a martial art would improve my health. I was thirty at the time and so desperate to feel better that if someone had suggested I hang by moon boots (a popular fad in the 1970s), I would have given it a good college try. But five years and one black belt later, I was just as sick as when I started. The psychic wasn't the only person who attempted to assist me in my quest for better health. Many kind and concerned people tried to help, and the providers they sent me to were *all* certain they could make a significant improvement to my health. They meant well and worked hard but failed, with one vital exception.

Complementary care used to be called alternative medicine but now goes by several names. The Mayo Clinic explains:

Exactly what's considered complementary and alternative medicine changes constantly as treatments undergo testing and move into the mainstream. To make sense of the many therapies available, it helps to look at how they're classified by the National Center for Complementary and Alternative Medicine (NCCAM), the agency that funds scientific research on complementary and alternative medicine:

- Whole medical systems
- Mind-body medicine
- Biologically based practices
- Manipulative and body-based practices
- Energy medicine

Keep in mind that the distinctions between therapies aren't always clear-cut, and some systems use techniques from more than one category.[14] Acupuncture, aromatherapy, yoga, and biofeedback are other examples of complementary care.

Many people living with illness feel Western medicine doesn't meet all their medical needs. Some of us have been upset or frustrated by our experiences with medical providers. We haven't forsaken Western medicine, but it has sometimes disappointed us. There are many pathways to improving our health. Utilizing complementary care is one of them. The absence of any definitive diagnosis for my health problems initially motivated my ventures into complementary care. No one could tell me what was wrong, so I focused my efforts on symptom reduction.

PHYSICAL THERAPIES

About a year after I began studying Tae Kwon Do, I started receiving regular acupuncture treatments. (This was prior to seeing an acupuncturist for my sinus issues.) The acupuncturist was a nice man, and he was sure he could restore me to good health. After a year of spending large sums of money on this treatment, I decided to stop going because the acupuncture hadn't made any significant change in my life.

I was also referred to a nutritionist, one who had been helpful to a relative suffering from severe allergies. The dynamic and upbeat nutritionist was certain if I followed the right food plan my health would improve. She put me on what I labeled the "Nuts and Grass Diet" because the plan eliminated so many major food groups, I felt as if all that remained was nuts and grass. Once into this new dietary routine, I actually liked the Nuts and Grass Diet, but it didn't help me feel much better. I continued to consult with the nutritionist and buy supplements from her, but after several years, even though I liked her, I could no longer justify the expense of the supplements. I stopped using her services.

I have a friend who is a Jin Shin Jyutsu practitioner. Jin Shin Jyutsu is an ancient Japanese healing technique similar to acupuncture but administered without needles. My friend was absolutely sure that through Jin Shin Jyutsu I would be restored to good health, and he encouraged me to give it a try. In a moment of desperation, I called a local practitioner and made an appointment. I saw two different practitioners over a two-and-a-half-year period, and I loved the work they did on me. I was very fond of these women and always felt good after my sessions. Unfortunately, Jin Shin Jyutsu did little to change my general health.

Despite the lack of desired results from these endeavors, I remain a strong advocate of complementary care. Each of the complementary care practices helped me a little. In addition, my experiences put me in the hands of people who were true healers, and in the case of my Tae Kwon Do master, a man who brought a Buddha-like serenity and strength into my life. These people made my life better even though they failed to heal me. At the time, I didn't feel particularly cared for by the medical community, but all of these practitioners and my Tae Kwon Do instructor made me feel they truly cared about me. They were all sincere in their efforts and beliefs, and I don't fault them for my illness being beyond their powers to cure. My ventures into complementary care were worth the time and money I spent even though none achieved what I initially hoped.

MEDITATION

Although my quest for good health via complementary care failed for a long time, I didn't give up. The search eventually brought me to the Mind Body Medical Institute (now called the Benson-Henry Institute for Mind Body Medicine, located at Massachusetts General Hospital,[15] where I took a multi-week course, as mentioned earlier. The first thing we learned in the course was how to elicit a relaxation response through a relaxation tape or meditation. Our initial homework assignment was to practice a relaxation response twice a day. At first I was annoyed with the assignment and couldn't believe how much of my precious free time I spent meditating, but after a couple weeks of twice-daily meditation, I began to feel better. I started the program the last week of November and by mid-December felt markedly healthier and more energized. I felt better in December than I had, collectively, all of the previous months of the year. I began to view meditation as wonderfully cheap medicine. More than a dozen years later, I continue to meditate regularly as if it were life-saving medication.

After I began to meditate, I found that I still became sick as often as I had in the past, but I recovered more quickly. Quick recovery was an entirely new experience for me. Before I began meditating, I often spent hours at my desk just trying to sit up so I could finish my work. With meditating, I still had bad spells days or weeks long, but work was seldom the daily endurance test it once had been. I'm convinced that meditation is the primary reason my health finally improved after three years of dramatically decreased functioning.

~

My history is a good argument for continuing to seek out complementary care. It took me a long time to find a practice that was effective, but when I did, it improved my life dramatically.

If you're interested in exploring complementary care options, you could inquire at your local community or senior center about low or no cost classes in yoga, nutrition, meditation, Tai Chi, etc. Most schools that teach complementary care practices will also offer free or low cost sessions so that their students may practice what they've learned. This might be a good way to expand your healthcare tool kit without incurring large expenses.

Using complementary care makes you less dependent on Western medicine, creating more balance in your life. If complementary care is disappointing, you can turn to your traditional doctor for help. If the traditional doctor doesn't meet your expectations, you'll have an alternative to fall back on. This helps to decrease feelings of frustration, helplessness, and dependency on either one system or the other. In addition, you may find yourself in the care of true healers, as I did.

Joanna J. Charnas, LICSW, LCSW

Part III
Financial and Legal Matters

Joanna J. Charnas, LICSW, LCSW

15

Money, Honey:
Public and Private Benefits

My long-time friend, Tom, fell the summer he was fifty-two, injuring his leg and back. The accident resulted in temporary incontinence and life-threatening surgery. When discharged from the hospital and back on his feet, he valiantly tried to resume his massage business, but he found traversing Manhattan with a walker challenging and stressful, especially when he used the subway. A couple of months after surgery, Tom informed me he'd decided to apply for social security. His work was too hard now and threatened his fragile health. I supported his decision; this is why we have public benefits.

The Federal government provides cash benefits and medical insurance to people who aren't able to work. Social Security (SSA) is available to people who've worked for at least ten years or forty work quarters. The amount of SSA is based on the length of your work history and the total funds you've contributed through payroll taxes. The other subsidy, Supplemental Security Income (SSI), is for people who've never worked or don't have forty quarters of employment history. These cash benefits don't depend on age but rather on disability and financial need. When you apply and are approved for SSA or SSI, you automatically become eligible for Medicare or Medicaid, respectively, two forms of federally subsidized health insurance.

SSA and SSI are available for people with physical and mental disabilities. To receive either, you must engage in a complex application process. You may begin the application via the Official Social Security Website[16] or at your local Social Security Office. Staff members are available at the office to guide you through your application if you need assistance.

If you were working when you became incapacitated, you may be eligible for private disability benefits through your employer. Most private disability insurance pays approximately sixty percent of the income you earned at the time you became disabled.

Social Security benefits are part of a network of federal entitlement programs. The important concept to remember about these programs is *you're entitled to them* if you meet the eligibility criteria. Rejection is common the first time you apply for SSA or SSI. Few people who apply know this. Sometimes, sick or disabled people must jump through numerous bureaucratic hoops before their benefits are approved. The Social Security Administration informed one of my friends that they lost her two-foot thick medical record. This happened twice. Another friend worked as a social worker at a large hospital for over twenty years. She believes her cancer patients were routinely denied SSA or SSI because Social Security personnel knew some of her patients would die before they could appeal their application denials.

When you apply for public or private benefits, it's important to learn your rights and know about the system with which you are dealing. Gather all of the application and eligibility information in writing and review it carefully to ensure that you understand it. Make copies for your files of the forms you submit. If this is too difficult a task to undertake by yourself, ask someone to help you navigate through the system (more about this in the next chapter).

~

The process to obtain financial and insurance benefits can be lengthy, so prepare for a long haul. Slog through whatever bureaucracies necessary because you deserve to receive the benefits to which you're entitled. A stable income and health insurance serve as a baseline to organize our financial lives and meet our basic needs.

Joanna J. Charnas, LICSW, LCSW

16

Speaking Up: Advocacy

Using an Advocate

In my wildest dreams, I never believed I'd ask for help from one of my elected officials. Many times, I'd seen people on the news who had done this. They'd tell their stories to the camera and thank their representatives in Congress or the Senate for righting some wrong in their lives in order to ensure their needs were met. But there I was, speaking to my state representative who'd offered to advocate for me.

All I wanted was a handicapped placard so I could conserve my energy on the days when I had next to none. I submitted an application along with my doctor's documentation of my CFS and physical limitations. I mailed it off and hoped for the best. Instead, I got the runaround. In response to my application, the Medical Affairs Branch of the Department of Motor Vehicles (DMV) requested I take a pulmonary test even though CFS doesn't cause pulmonary impairments. When I called the Medical Affairs Office to sort out the snafu, they also implied I had to be

Joanna J. Charnas, LICSW, LCSW

unable to walk to obtain a placard. I knew this was untrue based on my work with ambulatory AIDS patients. So, I called the Massachusetts CFIDS Association for guidance, and they advised me to call my state representative.

Initially, I dealt with Representative Tolman's aide. Ultimately Representative Tolman became personally involved because DMV personnel treated his aide rudely. After talking to me on the phone, he spoke to the Supervisor of the Medical Affairs Branch for the Massachusetts DMV, who told him point blank that I was ineligible. With some prodding and quotations from the state guidelines I had faxed him, Representative Tolman convinced the supervisor I *was* eligible for the placard. Because I asked for help from an elected official, the Massachusetts DMV approved my application.

ADVOCATING FOR YOUSELF

When you're sick, you may find yourself in situations like the one I had with the DMV. You'll need to advocate for yourself or enlist the help of someone who can advocate for you. You may be at odds with a medical provider, a public agency, or your employer. You might need to speak up for yourself in order to ensure you're receiving necessary medical care, the benefits you deserve, the enforcement of laws designed to protect you, and the appropriate assistance from government agencies.

Learning to state your needs clearly is important because they may not be obvious. You must learn to communicate them effectively. It may seem like a simple task, but often it isn't. This is particularly true when dealing with medical systems. For example, when I worked with the elderly, my colleagues and I frequently encountered clients who had absolute faith in and deep respect for their medical providers. These clients came from generations who never questioned their doctors' advice. Challenging a doctor was considered disrespectful. Sometimes, my clients didn't fully disclose their symptoms or inform their doctors when prescribed medications were ineffective. Blind faith and respect made more sense when people consulted family doctors who knew them well and treated them for decades.

This kind of unquestioning acceptance of our providers makes less sense when interacting with today's complex medical systems. We need to be mindful to *ask for* what we need from our doctors. If we don't think we're getting necessary care, we must ask for it firmly and repeatedly. If we're still dissatisfied with the care we receive, we should seek references for a different healthcare provider. For example, when I first asked my Health Maintenance Organization (HMO) to pay for the Mind Body Medical Program, my doctor told me the HMO wouldn't pay for it. He implied his hands were tied, so I began considering whether or not I could pay for the course myself. My friend Grace, who has multiple sclerosis, had taken their program for symptom reduction. When I told her my HMO refused to pay for the course, she advised me to call the Mind Body Medical Institute directly and talk to the person in charge of enrolling patients. I called this woman, who informed me my HMO *would* pay for the course and had done so for other patients who belonged to the same HMO.

I called my doctor back and relayed this information to him. I made a long, heartfelt argument about my need for this course. Part of my plea must have affected him because he offered to call someone at the HMO who might be able to approve my request. After his call on my behalf, I would also need to make my case directly to her.

A few days later, I was able to speak to the woman in question. When she finally agreed to have the HMO foot the fourteen-hundred-dollar bill, I was so relieved I started to cry the minute I hung up the phone.

This isn't a story of a bad doctor or a bad HMO, but I had to advocate for myself repeatedly. I didn't become upset or emotional with my doctor when he initially denied my request. Instead I remained firm, clear, and relentless until I received what I needed. Advocating effectively for myself isn't a skill I developed quickly or easily. I'm ordinarily an emotional person, but being emotional wouldn't have served me well in that situation. It took all my force of will and self-control to advocate calmly and persuasively.

Advocating for yourself is something you learn to do well through practice. It's not only okay, it's essential, so you must learn to be fearless. Denial of something necessary to your fundamental well-being can be painful. Don't let pain or anger get in the way of your goal. Focus on being clear about your objectives and calm in your presentation. Use notes if needed. Be persistent. You're taking care of your health, so don't give up.

~

ASKING OTHER PEOPLE TO ADVOCATE FOR YOU

Sometimes you'll decide to advocate for yourself, but other times it makes more sense to have someone else advocate on your behalf. You might want a trusted friend, partner, or relative to speak for you. If you can't think clearly or explain fully what you're experiencing, someone close to you may be a better advocate than you are. If you're very sick, you may not have the stamina to advocate for yourself. I have a friend who takes her wife with her to all her medical appointments. It's fine to have a loved one advocate for you as long as you trust this person and believer she will be more effective than you can be.

Sometimes we need other people to advocate for us because they have more power or authority. I'm convinced that without the advocacy of my state representative, I wouldn't have been able to obtain a handicapped placard. In this case, having an advocate with clout was essential to accomplishing my goal.

It's likely you'll need the help of an advocate sometime in the course of managing your illness. Learn to advocate for yourself as best you can, but don't feel that you have to do all of it yourself. Enlist the help of anyone you need, as I did when I dealt with the DMV. No matter how you choose to proceed, don't hesitate to fight for what you need and deserve.

Joanna J. Charnas, LICSW, LCSW

17

You Have Rights:
Important Laws That Protect You

I panicked. I'd worked for the Naval Hospital for two years as a contract employee, and now my job had been reclassified as a federal position. As a result, I needed to apply for the same position I'd held for two years if I wanted to keep my job. The formal hiring process for a federal employee involved a thorough physical by the Occupational Health Department at the hospital. I would have to disclose my Chronic Fatigue Syndrome (CFS), and I feared my illness would disqualify me, leaving me unemployed. To assuage my panic, I gave myself a crash course in the Americans with Disabilities Act,[17] commonly known as the ADA. As I had hoped, the crash course confirmed that my new employer couldn't disqualify me based solely on my diagnosis. I learned Title V of the Rehabilitation Act of 1973 covered my rights as an applicant for a position in the federal government. This act preceded the ADA and is the model for it.

It's important to become familiar with the two federal laws created to safeguard the rights of people living with disabilities and illness. These laws can make your life easier during times of declining health or a health crisis.

FAMILY MEDICAL LEAVE ACT

The first law is the Family Medical Leave Act,[18] often referred to as FMLA, which Congress passed in 1993. It gives people the right to take up to 12 weeks of leave per year for the birth or adoption of a child or for recovery from a serious health condition of the employee or a member of the employee's immediate family.

Eligibility

A serious health condition can be a physical or mental illness and includes addiction treatment. In order to be eligible for the Family Medical Leave (FML), you must have worked for your employer for at least twelve months, but I've seen employers grant FML to colleagues who had not worked twelve months yet as acts of kindness or in order to retain valued staff.

This law only applies to employers who have fifty or more staff. So, when I look for new jobs, I'm careful about where I apply. Given my history of CFS relapses and frequent, severe colds, I know I might need to utilize FML in the future. Therefore, I only seek employment from large agencies. If you're currently working, review your employee handbook carefully. It should state your employer's FMLA policy. It's always wise to be well versed in your employee handbook, but it's even more important when we live with a chronic illness or disability.

Right to Privacy

One important aspect of the FMLA is your right to privacy. The law protects you from disclosing an illness to your employer unless you choose to do so. You'll probably

need a doctor's note if you're sick for more than a desig-
nated time (usually three to five days), but the note only
has to verify that you require time off for medical purpos-
es. It does *not* need to specify your illness. In most work
environments, it's illegal for your employer to ask you to
identify your illness. When I worked as a supervisor, I was
always extremely careful about what I said to staff regarding their health, even if they'd disclosed their illnesses to
me. I was wary of saying anything an employee might mis-
construe as discriminatory. This is not a bad thing. The
law protecting my staff protected me as well.

PROTECTION FROM DISCRIMINATION

The second important law is the ADA, mentioned
above. Congress created the law in 1990 to protect people
living with disabilities from discrimination "in employment, state and local government services, public accommodations, commercial facilities, and transportation."

The ADA website includes this information: "Employers with 25 or more employees were covered as of July 26,
1992. Employers with 15 or more employees were covered
two years later, beginning July 26, 1994."[19]

REASONABLE ACCOMMODATION

The ADA allows employees with disabilities to ask for
"reasonable accommodations" in the work place. A reasonable accommodation might include a flexible work schedule to allow time for medical treatment or special equip-
ment to assist an employee in doing his job. For example,
if part of a nurse's job is to chart, but she has carpel tunnel
syndrome, she might ask for a Dictaphone and record her
charting notes orally. She could then have someone else
write or type them for her. Or if a cancer patient must receive radiation therapy early every morning, he might ask

to change his work schedule to accommodate treatments. The employee must request the accommodation because employers are not obligated to identify staff needs and respond. They are only obligated to respond *after* an employee has requested an accommodation.

Not all requested accommodations are reasonable. When I supervised an elder protection program (similar to child protection, but for the elderly), my staff had to visit the homes of each alleged victim and observe the home setting. I once interviewed a job applicant who was blind. She didn't have the capacity to make these observations. To accommodate her blindness, the agency would have required another employee to accompany her on home visits in order to make the observations *for her*. In other words, someone else would have performed this essential job function, creating an unreasonable accommodation.

If You're Refused...

If you believe an employer has violated your rights under the ADA, you may file a written complaint with the Equal Employment Opportunity Commission (EEOC)[20] within 180 days after the violation took place. If your employer doesn't respond to your complaints, you may also want to hire an attorney to represent you.

~

The ADA and FMLA make me feel protected at work. If you aren't familiar with these laws, I encouraged you to learn about them. They're your best protection in the work place when you live with chronic illness.

Part IV
Spiritual Considerations

Joanna J. Charnas, LICSW, LCSW

18

Keeping the Faith

Alone in my car and overcome by sadness, with two hours of dark road ahead before I would reach home, I prayed. I bargained with God. I told him if he would help me, I'd do my part to get better. In that moment of prayer, I felt love, comfort, and relief. It was one of the most meaningful experiences of my life.

Becoming sick is an open invitation from the universe to get to know the Almighty better. If you don't currently have a relationship with a force or being you believe is divine, ask yourself if you want this in your life. If you have a pre-existing relationship with God, now that you are ill, consider if you want to deepen that relationship. Whether you are a Christian, Muslim, Jew Buddhist, of another faith, undecided, or currently of no faith, a strong spiritual presence may bring you solace. You never have to be alone, and in your worst moments, like mine, you'll always have someone to turn to. God will provide you with understanding and love. I can't imagine my life without Him at its center.

Joanna J. Charnas, LICSW, LCSW

One of my spiritual role models, my friend John, says, "God is good all the time." The simplicity and purity of this idea profoundly affects my life, and I keep it with me all the time, like the security blanket of a three-year-old, well used and much loved. I trust this is true. At my sickest or most scared, remembering this article of faith is challenging, but I always return to it.

Prayer and meditation are instruments through which we communicate with God. I believe in practicing prayer because if it's a habit, then when you need to talk to God, you already know how to do it. Then, prayer will flow naturally. Because I'm in the practice of praying, when I have a crisis I find that I pray automatically. If nothing else, it calms and centers me.

Sometimes, I'm too upset or sick to summon the mental concentration formulating prayers requires. At those times, I recite existing prayers. I'm particularly fond of the serenity prayer and *Psalm Twenty-Three*. Sometimes, all I can do is say them over and over. Even at my worst moments, this practice is soothing and helpful.

When I formulate my own prayers, I pray for guidance and strength. Equally important, I pray for others. Praying for others is empowering. No matter how disabled I am, as long as I can think clearly, I have the power to pray for the well-being of other people. I strongly believe in the power of this practice; it helps me be less self-absorbed. During the initial stages of my divorce, a friend's daughter received a diagnosis of life-threatening cancer. I tried to remember her, always, in my prayers. I was thrilled when the daughter went into remission and pleased that during a difficult time in my life, I'd been a part of something good outside of myself.

I also pray in gratitude. This practice may seem like a stretch for you if you're living in constant pain or if illness has imposed numerous obstacles to what you once envisioned as a happy life, but be grateful for what you still have. On my worst days, I'm grateful for my friends and family, my crazy cats, the home I've lived in for a dozen years, dark chocolate, good movies, and so many other things.

In my late twenties, I decided I could distill everything meaningful in my life into beauty, love, and growth. Even at my sickest, I wake up each morning grateful to God for the possibility of these three elements gracing my day. Figure out what you're grateful for and consider expressing gratitude for these things when you pray or meditate.

~

Belief in a higher power can make all the difference in your life as you struggle with illness, often when nothing or no one else is able to. Some of the most moving moments of my life have been the ones I've shared alone with God. I feel watched over and loved. You can have this in your life too, and it may provide you with the comfort and solace I feel.

Joanna J. Charnas, LICSW, LCSW

19

I Am What I Am:
Defining Ourselves

One of the most famous people living in the United States with Chronic Fatigue Syndrome is Laura Hillenbrand, who wrote the bestsellers *Seabiscuit: An American Legend* (2001) and *Unbroken: A World War II Story of Survival, Resilience, and Redemption* (2010). CFS is so disabling for her that she rarely leaves her home. She's a person who lives with a debilitating chronic illness, but she's so much more. If you'd like to learn more about this writer, visit BeliefNet[21] on the Web.

It's important to remember our illness is not the entirety of who we are. For six years, I worked on the psychiatry wards at the hospital where I'm currently employed. I counseled numerous patients who'd just been diagnosed with a serious mental illness (usually bi-polar disorder or schizophrenia) and consequently learned they needed to stay on medication for the rest of their lives. I frequently had some version of the following conversation:

"Do I have to stay on this medication forever?"

"Yes, you do if you want to remain healthy."

"But I don't want to be sick forever."

After I helped them process their feelings, I would look around the psychiatry ward and comment, "You know, there are three people who work on this ward who park in the handicapped parking lot. Can you tell who they are?"

"No, I can't."

"So, they don't wear big signs saying they're sick or handicapped?"

"No, they don't."

"But they are. Maybe you can learn to live with your mental illness and manage it so well no one will be able to tell either."

This is always an eye-opening idea for young people who have recently received a diagnosis of a lifelong mental illness. They often can't see past their diagnoses and toward a meaningful life. Helping patients understand they weren't just their new diagnosis was an important part of my job. I tried to break down their "them/us" thinking and accept that the divisions they created for themselves, making them feel less than complete, were only in their heads. There is no them/us. There is only us.

Before I worked at a nursing home in my mid-forties, the phrase "differently abled" always struck me as a revolting, politically correct platitude. My thoughts about this phrase changed after I ran a support group there. The age of my group members ranged from early twenties to early sixties. The group participants had a staggering array of debilitating diagnoses. Two had paranoid schizophrenia. Two were drug addicts. Three were quadriplegic and used electric wheelchairs. One of the group members was developmentally delayed, meaning his IQ was below seventy. He also had AIDS and an assault record.

Judging the members only by their diagnoses, they shouldn't have formed a cohesive and effective support group, but they surprised me by evolving into the best group I had ever led. One of the members with schizophrenia was still occasionally psychotic. Somehow, he managed to offer the most profound insights expressed. The developmentally delayed member was also savvy and street smart. He could get to the root of any issue almost immediately and with startling clarity. The participants were all able to do the hard work of a support group. They spoke openly and honestly about their personal issues, listened respectfully, and supported each other with wisdom and compassion.

As I sat with these people week after week, I began to admire them for all their strengths and abilities and to forget about their illnesses and disabilities. Their electric wheelchairs became no more than reasonable substitutes for walking. The group members didn't seem disabled to me when we sat in group together. The term "differently abled" stopped sounding like drivel and began to make sense. The participants seemed whole and beautiful exactly as they were.

We are also beautiful and whole exactly as we are. We aren't more or less than other people. All human beings face distinct personal challenges as they go through life. The famed Broadway actress Elaine Stritch, in the documentary *Elaine Stritch: Shoot Me* (2013), sums this up succinctly by saying, "Everyone has a bag of rocks." Some of our challenges involve physical or mental health, but we are no less whole because of our challenges than the middle-aged woman going through a divorce, the laid-off thirty-year-old man, or the student who becomes desperately confused in the middle of college. Our challenges are simply more quantifiable or visible. But we're still complete unto ourselves and should never feel that we are less than perfect versions of ourselves.

~

We *are* perfect just the way we are.

20

Unexpected Gifts

Living with illness doesn't just change how we must live our life; it also changes our outlook on life. No one I know who is living with illness would choose to be sick. For some of us, though, the challenges have provided us with gifts we didn't anticipate. The gifts don't make up for the disruption and pain that we've experienced, but ignoring the gifts serves no purpose. Embracing them gives some meaning to what we've experienced through illness.

DEVELOPMENT OF EMOTIONAL HEALTH

Being sick clarified how I want to live my life. I place a much stronger value on living in the moment, although I'm frequently unsuccessful at embodying this maxim. For years, my health often changed from hour to hour, and I still can never count on feeling well beyond the moment. When I tie myself in emotional knots, I know I'm wasting precious good health by being upset. Being physically sick gives me powerful motivation for being as emotionally healthy as possible. I learned this particular lesson during my three-year relapse.

DEVELOPMENT OF GREATER FAITH

My illness also deepened my faith and brought me closer to God. This happened not because I got better, but because at my sickest I felt I could always turn to God for help.

IMPROVEMENT OF RELATIONSHIPS

Being sick broadened my view of relationships. I understand much better now that most issues between people aren't black or white but infinitesimal shades of gray. Illness brought me closer to some of my loved ones and helped me be more accepting of the limitations of others. It's taught me to be more forgiving than I used to be because I don't want to waste time and energy being angry.

SELF-CONFIDENCE

Illness also helped me learn that I'm much tougher than I formerly believed. It's enhanced my sense of self-competence. I'm proud of the fortitude I developed in making sure my needs were met. I never gave up the fight to improve my health or the hope that it would improve. I've had several ardent cheerleaders and at least a couple of great advocates, but my health improved from my own efforts. Remembering that I've successfully worked through many of the challenges my illness created gives me confidence that I can work through whatever new obstacles I face.

~

Illness colors every day of my life, but the unexpected gifts I gained from being sick also color every day. I don't seek meaning in illness, but I accept that it has given meaning to my life in unanticipated ways. I treasure the gifts illness has bestowed on me. If you're suffering, you may struggle to appreciate the good that has come from something that feels wholly bad. In your quietest moments though, seek out the unexpected gifts. You've suffered for them and deserve to acknowledge and embrace them.

Whether you like it or not, you've been given a life that includes illness. You can choose to face it with courage and fortitude. Live each day doing your best at whatever you attempt, and be proud of your efforts. Fight the battles you need to, and laugh at yourself at every opportunity. Continue to live with as much zest as possible. Most important of all, always believe that a happy life is within your grasp.

Joanna J. Charnas, LICSW, LCSW

End Notes

1. http://www.webmd.com/

2. http://www.cdc.gov/

3. http://www.mayoclinic.org

4. http://www.nami.org

5. http://www.masscfids.org

6. https://www.presidentschallenge.org/informed/digest/docs/200112digest.pdf

7. http://www.hsph.harvard.edu/nutritionsource/pyramid-full-story/

8. http://sleepfoundation.org/

9. http://www.mayoclinic.org/meditation/art-20045858

10. http://www.bensonhenryinstitute.org/about/our-store

11. http://www.drweil.com/drw/u/ART00581/water-an-essential-part-of-life.html

12. http://www.care.com

13. http://www.exhibithealth.com/general-health/health-benefits-of-human-touch-1345/

14. http://www.mayoclinic.org/healthy-living/consumer-health/in-depth/alternative-medicine/art-20045267

15. http://www.massgeneral.org/bhi/

16. https://www.ssa.gov

17. http://www.ada.gov

18. http://www.dol.gov/whd/fmla/

19. http://www.ada.gov/employmt.htm

20. http://www.eeoc.gov/

21. http://www.beliefnet.com/Health/Health-Support/
    Illness-and-Recovery/What-Price-Glory.aspx#

References

Books

Comfort, Alex. 2009. *The joy of sex: The ultimate revised edition.* New York, NY: Crown Publishers.

Durstine, J. Larry, Geoffrey Moore, Patricia Painter, and Scott Roberts, eds. 2009. *American College of Sports Medicine's Exercise management for persons with chronic disease and disabilities.* Champaign, IL: Human Kinetics.

Fisher, Helen. 1994. *The anatomy of love: A natural history of mating, marriage, and why we stray.* New York, NY: Ballantine Books.

Greenberger, Dennis and Christine A. Padesky. 1995. *Mind over mood: Change how you feel by changing the way you think.* New York, NY: The Guilford Press.

Hillenbrand, Laura. 2001. *Seabiscuit: An American legend.* New York, NY: Random House.

Hillenbrand, Laura. 2010. *Unbroken: A World War II story of survival, resilience, and redemption.* New York, NY: Random House.

Pizzorno, Joseph E. and Michael T. Murray. 2006. Stress management. *Textbook of natural medicine,* 701–708. St. Louis, MO: Churchill Livingstone.

Stoll, Walt and Jan DeCourtney. 2006. *Recapture your health: Management for persons with chronic diseases and disabilities.* Boulder, CO: Sunrise Health Coach Publications.

The Oxford Dictionary of Quotations. (5th ed.). 1999. Edited by Elizabeth Knowles. Oxford, NY: Oxford University Press.

FILMS

Jimenez, Neal. *The Waterdance.* Directors Neal Jiminez and Michael Steinberg. 1992. USA: No Frills Film Production. Video release: 2001.

Meriwether, Elizabeth and Michael Samonek. *No Strings Attached.* Director Ivan Reitman. 2011. USA: Paramount Pictures. Video release: 2011.

Merryman, Keith, David A. Newman, Will Gluck, and Harley Peyton. *Friends with Benefits.* Director Will Gluck. 2011. USA: Screen Gems.

Stritch, Elaine. *Shoot Me.* Documentary. Director Chiemi Karasawa. 2013. USA: Isotope Films. Video release: 2014.

Other Books by MSI Press

A Believer-in-Waiting's First Encounters with God (Mahlou)

Blest Atheist (Mahlou)

El Poder de lo Transpersonal (Ustman)

Forget the Goal, the Journey Counts (Stites)

Joshuanism (Tosto)

Losing My Voice and Finding Another (Thompson)

Metaphors of Islamic Humanism (O. Imady)

Of God, Rattlesnakes, and Okra (Easterling)

Publishing for Smarties (Ham)

Puertas a la Eternidad (Ustman)

Road to Damascus (E. Imady)

Syrian Folktales (M. Imady)

The Gospel of Damascus (O. Imady)

The Marriage Whisperer (Pickett)

The Rose and the Sword (Bach and Hucknall)

The Seven Wisdoms of Life (Tubali)

The Widower's Guide to a New Life (Romer)

Thoughts without a Title (Henderson)

Understanding the People Around You (Filatova)

Widow: A Survival Guide for the First Year (Romer)

CPSIA information can be obtained at www.ICGtesting.com
Printed in the USA
LVOW07s1955120116

470314LV00013B/216/P